Have Co-Teaching and Collaboration in the Classroom

Practical Strategies for Success

Second Edition

Susan Gingras Fitzell, M.Ed.

Co-Teaching and Collaboration in the Classroom
2nd Edition

If you have questions or would like customized school in-service or ongoing consultation, contact:
Susan Gingras Fitzell
PO Box 6182
Manchester, NH 03108-6182
Phone: 603-625-6087 or 210-473-2863
Email: SFitzell@SusanFitzell.com

Main Website: http://www.SusanFitzell.com
Interactive Blog & Teacher Resource:
http://www.HighTestScores.org
Facebook: http://www.facebook.com/SusanFitzellfb
YouTube: http://www.youtube.com/susanfitzell
Twitter: http://twitter.com/susanfitzell
For supplemental handouts and information:
www.aimhieducational.com/inclusion.aspx

At the time of publication, the information cited within is the most current available and/or the original source material. The author and publisher do not provide any guarantee or warranty regarding the information provided by any sources cited here, nor do we take responsibility for any changes to information or Web sites. If you find an error or would like to alert us to a change to any resource cited herein, please contact us online: http://aimhieducational.com/ContactUs.asp. We encourage parents and teachers to closely monitor Internet usage by children and students.

Other selected titles by Susan Gingras Fitzell, M.Ed.:

Special Needs In The General Classroom: Strategies That Make It Work

Paraprofessionals and Teachers Working Together

Umm Studying? What's That?: Learning Strategies for the Overwhelmed and Confused College and High School Student

Please Help Me With My Homework! Strategies for Parents and Caregivers

Transforming Anger to Personal Power: An Anger Management Curriculum for Grades 6 through 12

Free the Children: Conflict Education for Strong & Peaceful Minds

DEDICATION

This book is dedicated to Ed Burgess, my co-teaching partner. Thanks for always being positive and supportive even through the rough times. We were truly a co-teaching TEAM. I will always be grateful to you for doing your best to make inclusion work.

Also, thanks to my ever-so-patient family, Mike, Shivahn, and Ian, for encouraging me to fulfill my passion: to help teachers all over the world make a difference for ALL our children.

TABLE OF CONTENTS

Part 1: Co-Teaching Basics

What is Co-Teaching?

Co-teaching is two or more teachers working together to provide instruction, typically, to students in an inclusive setting. Within a true co-teaching model, teachers plan together, instruct the class together, and collaborate with grading and differentiating instruction. In an ideal educational setting, teachers have common planning time to support their work in the inclusive classroom. Co-teaching allows educators to meet the needs of at-risk students, those who are not responding, gifted, or with disabilities who may be struggling in the classroom. In a co-teaching classroom that fully utilizes the talents of the two teachers and any other adult staff in the room, students are more likely to achieve high standards, to be successful, and to behave more appropriately than they would in segregated pull-out or self-contained classrooms.

When I first started co-teaching, I firmly believed that it was a set-up for failure for students with learning disabilities in the general classroom. I did not believe that the students on my caseload would be able to handle the academic challenges of a general education classroom. I also had significant concerns that my collaborative teachers would not understand the needs of students on an IEP and consequently would not teach in such a way that they could be successful. Within the first year of co-teaching, I realized that even if the situation was not ideal, there were some benefits. The first benefit of including students with special needs and behavioral problems in the general classroom was that their behavior significantly improved when surrounded by positive peer role models. The second benefit was that the bar had been raised and, when provided with proper supports and learning strategies, students with special needs not only rose to the challenge, they also gained the benefit of having more resources available to them in the general education classroom.

In a co-teaching situation, students not only have the benefit of a content expert providing instruction, they have the benefits of a learning strategies expert to provide necessary scaffolding, adaptations, accommodations, interventions, and modifications.

What is Not Co-Teaching?

Co-teaching is NOT tag team teaching. For example, sometimes teachers in a co-teaching situation split the instruction so that while one person is teaching the other is planning lessons, making copies, running errands, correcting papers, or doing any number of things that are not providing instruction or supporting the instruction of the teacher up front.

Co-teaching is NOT one teacher teaching while the other teacher holds up the wall or decorates a desk. Co-teaching requires that both certified teachers are involved in providing instruction or direct support to student learning in the classroom.

Co-teaching is NOT when two subject area teachers or two grade level teachers combine their classes to teach a lesson, a unit, or a project together. This scenario is called team teaching and has a research base primarily in the humanities. Co-teaching is not a term for interdisciplinary instruction.

Co-teaching is NOT inclusion and inclusion is not co-teaching. In many areas of the country there is a marriage of these terms where they are used interchangeably. However, inclusion refers to a philosophy and practice where all students – gifted, learning-disabled, and of mixed ability are in the same classroom as a learning community. Co-teaching is only one way to implement inclusion.

Co-teaching is NOT general education teachers working with a special education teacher who is in and out of the classroom inconsistently, and consequently does not have a realistic way to deliver instruction, plan with the classroom teacher, share responsibilities in the classroom on a regular basis, or in any other way be a person in the room, but not someone the general education teacher can count on. When students with special needs are included in the general education classroom and classroom teachers are assigned a special educator who is not actually scheduled in that specific classroom a minimum of two days a week, the special education teacher is acting as a consultant within a collaboration model.

Special education teacher as consultant

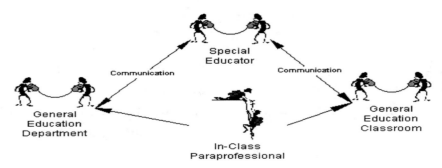

In this inclusion model the special education teacher acts as 'consultant' to the general classroom teacher. The special education 'consultant' works primarily outside the classroom with the general education teacher and may work directly in classrooms as needed. The general classroom teacher in this situation makes most, if not all, of the classroom adaptations, accommodations, and modifications using the Individual Education Plan (IEP) and the special educator is available as a guide and resource. If a paraprofessional is assigned to the general classroom, the special education teacher works closely with both the paraprofessional and the general classroom teacher. While this model is a good way to implement inclusion, it is <u>not</u> co-teaching.

Who Can Co-Teach?

During a recent seminar on the topic of inclusion strategies, two women came up to me with huge concerns about the co-teaching initiative their district was starting. I was astounded when I was told that they were paraprofessionals rather than certified teachers. They were very uncomfortable with what was being asked of them by their building principal, however, they did not feel they had the power to challenge the district decision to have paraprofessionals in a co-teaching role.

Paraprofessionals can re-teach or implement a lesson plan written by a certified teacher, under the supervision of a certified teacher. However, a paraprofessional is not qualified to co-teach, nor does the paraprofessional receive a salary commensurate with the responsibility of teaching. Paraprofessionals are employed as non-certified personnel. This directly affects what responsibilities they should have in the classroom. Co-teaching is a service delivery system which requires two or more certified teachers or licensed staff to collaborate and provide instruction to the diverse classroom. The bottom line is that certified teachers and the licensed staff co-teach and paraprofessionals support in the classroom.

Benefits of Co-Teaching

- Facilitates successful transition into the general classroom
- Reduces teacher stress and burnout
- Increases student achievement
- Models collaborative relationships
- Two teaching styles is a benefit to all students
- Eases burden on the general classroom teacher
- Easier for specialists to follow-up with students

Should Co-Teaching Be Voluntary?

When a co-teaching program is a new initiative for a district, it is best to start small and with teachers who are willing, if possible. By using this approach, a school can work out major issues before going full-scale. This strategy works well because any anxiety teachers have before implementation of the program will only be exacerbated if the program is started too much, too fast, without proper preparation or training, or with unwilling teachers. Any problems that occur become fuel for the argument that co-teaching doesn't work.

Ideally, school districts start the co-teaching initiative with teachers who are willing to take on the challenge and immerse themselves in professional development geared toward making co-teaching a success. Sometimes schools have no choice but to assign teachers to a co-teaching role, even when unwilling, because of the need to meet IEP requirements or state standards. In this situation, try to carefully match up personalities for the best possible success. Co-teaching is like an arranged marriage, and the personalities sharing a classroom can make or break the co-teaching relationship. All the conflict resolution or professionalism in the world cannot compensate for two seriously mismatched personalities.

If the district is struggling to find co-teaching matches, teachers may need to be moved to different grade levels or lose preferred schedules so that teachers who are willing to co-teach can work together.

Where Does Co-Teaching Take Place?

I was coaching at a middle school where the co-teaching initiative was very new and teachers had very little training on how to co-teach effectively. About 10 minutes into one class period, the special education teacher called a group of students up to join her and they proceeded to leave the room. When I was debriefing the teachers later in the day, they explained that because there was such a wide range of abilities in the classroom, they found it easier to divide the class and pull out the students with special needs for separate instruction. Upon further questioning it became clear that this was a regular practice. This is not co-teaching. This is a pull-out program. Although it may seem to be a sensible approach to managing wide gaps and ability levels in the classroom, any benefit of a co-teaching environment is lost when students with special needs are pulled out. While students with special needs are not in the classroom they are missing out on positive peer role models, higher-order thinking from group discussion, and interaction between their teachers. They may also miss out on instruction they will need for classroom assessments or their state test.

Co-teaching usually takes place in one classroom. Different ability levels can be addressed through flexible grouping, Acceleration Centers™, tiered lesson plans, mixed-ability groups, and occasional same-ability groups. Only in very specific situations, such as oral testing, is it appropriate to take some students out of the room.

Sometimes when co-teachers are alternative-teaching it may be appropriate and desirable to take some students out of the room. For example, one teacher might remain in the classroom and teach poetry while the other teacher takes students to the computer room to write an essay. Halfway through the period the students switch. In another scenario, some students are reading and need quiet, while other students are working on a project that requires talking and activity.

When students with special needs are pulled out for specific instruction, a Response to Intervention (RTI) action, or for skill-building, be cautious about regularly including students without an Individual Education Plan (IEP) in the pull-out group. It is important not to give the impression that general education students are receiving special education without proper assessment, documentation, eligibility determination, and placement procedures being followed. It is critical that students don't miss out on a 'least restrictive environment' by being pulled out of the general classroom unnecessarily.

How Many Days a Week Should We Co-Teach?

When I first started co-teaching, I was in the classroom every single day with my co-teacher, working the instructional process. Co-teaching on a daily basis provided consistency, an understanding of day-to-day classroom dynamics, the ability for us to follow through with lesson plans and necessary supports together, and a thorough knowledge of what was happening with each student on a day-to-day basis. Daily co-teaching is the ideal co-teaching situation. Most schools, however, because of shortages in staffing, numbers of students with special needs, and limited or restrictive schedules, find it difficult to assign teachers to a classroom every day. Consequently, special education teachers are often spread between several classes over the course of two or three days.

When I was co-teaching on a daily basis, the percentage of students on an IEP in the general education classroom could be almost 50%. Because of this high percentage, the district decided to spread students with special needs out amongst more classes so that no teacher had more than 25% of their class population with special needs. In order to accomplish this, special education teachers were assigned to one class two days a week and another class three days a week. This model may have been more inclusive, but it was much more difficult to co-teach. Co-teaching, when not done on a daily basis, can be successful if teachers plan carefully for the days that the co-teacher is present and use strategies such as Acceleration Centers or flexible grouping on those days. Teachers should try to plan activities for the days the co-teacher is present that take full advantage of having another certified teacher in the room.

One unintended consequence of having a special education teacher assigned to so many classrooms in a co-teaching environment is often a lack of time to plan with the co-teacher. The time that a special education teacher is assigned to a classroom should be held sacred. Special educators should not be pulled away from the general education classroom for crises, IEP meetings, or other random duties. If time to meet for IEPs is an issue, or the special educator needs time for assessments and other professional responsibilities, it might be best to schedule him or her in the classroom four days a week and allow one day a week for work outside the classroom. Co-teaching works best when applied daily.

Co-Teaching Approaches

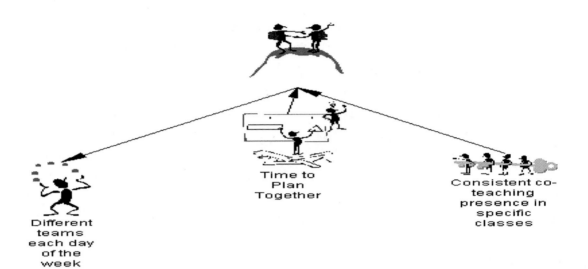

Time to Plan Together

Different teams each day of the week

Consistent co-teaching presence in specific classes

One Teacher, One Support Teacher • Subject expert often lead teacher • Support teacher often specialist	Support teacher's role defined by IEPs. The more time spent planning and collaborating, the more benefit to all in the classroom.
Parallel Teaching • Divide the class in half • Both teach the same content to smaller group • Plan together for consistency	It's important to not be hierarchical and to divide the student mix carefully so that both groups have a variety of students that work well together.
Alternative Teaching • Usually one large group & one smaller group • May teach the same or different content • Each teach their content, then switch	This is a good approach to use as needed. Having several small groups for different purposes would also eliminate some of the stigma of the L.D. student always being singled out.
Team Teaching • Shared instruction and planning • Coordinated activities and dialog • Trust, commitment, and personality compatibility a must	Many see this situation as the ideal; however, it requires two teachers who are compatible in personality style, commitment, and teaching philosophy, who are also given the time and support to plan together.
Station Teaching* - Advanced Co-Teaching • Acceleration Centers™ • Flexible groups, individual instruction	This approach is one of the most effective formats for addressing a wide range of abilities in the general education classroom. See "Advanced Co-Teaching: Station Teaching" (pg. 27) for more information.

* The definition of Station Teaching in this book is different from other resources. This text attempts to differentiate between Parallel Teaching, Alternative Teaching, and Station Teaching more distinctly, as well as taking co-teaching to the next level through flexible grouping and Fitzell Acceleration Centers.

What Co-Teaching Approaches Don't Look Like

One teacher, one support teacher does not look like:

- One teaches and the other does the grading, the copying, and the paperwork.
- One teaches and the other teacher sits in the classroom, unsure of what to do because there's been no communication, spending his or her time feeling a lack of ownership and involvement in the teaching process.
- One teacher teaches while the other teacher works in the background, monitoring students, pointing students in the right direction, and helping students, yet never being involved in more than those activities and feeling like he or she has no authority to contribute to the lesson plan or make on-the-spot accommodations, adaptations, or interventions.

Station teaching does not look like:

- All the gifted students are together, all the average students are together, and all the special education students are together.
- Only the special education students or the gifted students get to do the stations.
- The classroom teacher single-handedly creates the station and the special education teacher isn't sure of what's going on or how they work.

Parallel teaching does not look like:

- The students on an IEP are with the special education teacher and all the other students are with the general education teacher (most of the time).
- A special education teacher is given a lesson plan and has no authority to make accommodations and adaptations as necessary.

Alternative teaching does not look like:

- The groups of students with the special education teacher are always the students on an IEP.
- A special education teacher is given a lesson plan and has no authority to make accommodations and adaptations as necessary.

Team teaching does not look like:

- Tag team teaching... My turn, your turn.
- One teacher teaches while the other teacher uses the time as a prep period.

Next, let's take a look at descriptions of the five co-teaching models, the benefits and challenges of each model, as well as consider examples of each model and what co-teaching *DOES* look like.

One Teacher, One Support Teacher

In the **'one teacher, one support'** model, one teacher has the primary responsibility for planning and teaching while the other teacher supports students, the learning process, and the classroom teacher.

Let's consider the increasing demand on teachers to implement data-driven decision-making. When using the **'one teacher, one support'** model, the supporting teacher is in a good position to observe students and collect data. It is difficult for a single teacher to teach as well as collect observational data at the same time. Co-teachers can work together in advance to decide what types of information to collect, how to collect that information, and how they might use it to make adjustments in the classroom.

While one teacher is teaching, the other teacher can circulate through the room, provide assistance to individual students, use position control to manage behavior, consider ways to reinforce the current lesson later, put notes on the board, and ask questions for the students that they might not ask on their own.

Benefits of One Teacher, One Support Teacher
- Students receive individual help in a timely manner.
- It's easier to keep students on track.
- The model allows for student observation and data collection.
- Each teacher brings his or her own perspective into the lesson.
- Although co-planning is required and strongly recommended, this model requires minimal co-planning.

Challenges of One Teacher, One Support Teacher
- Students may consider one teacher as the 'real' teacher and the other teacher as the teacher's aide.
- The second teacher's activity in the classroom might be distracting, or considered distracting to the students or the other teacher.
- Students may begin to expect immediate personal assistance, especially if the class is structured so that all students with special needs are seated together with the special education teacher in close proximity and easily available for immediate help.

What Can We Actually Do in a Co-Taught Classroom?

The following chart is helpful when planning lessons and working out roles and responsibilities in the co-taught classroom. It offers many options for what the 'other' teacher in the room can do.

Co-teacher #1 is	Co-teacher #2 is
Direct teaching whole class lesson	<ul><li>Writing notes on the board or overhead</li><li>Constantly looking for ways to present what the general education teacher is teaching visually or differently:</li><li>Creating posters</li><li>Creating self-playing PowerPoint presentations that review information</li><li>Creating handouts with visuals as a supplement or addendum</li><li>Circulating to check understanding and notes completion</li><li>Observing student response to plan for future groupings</li><li>Monitoring student understanding to suggest future accommodations</li><li>Repeating or clarifying difficult concepts</li><li>Using position control for behavior management</li><li>Considering enrichment opportunities</li><li>Running last-minute copies or errands (use this option sparingly)</li><li>Completing behavior documentation charts, doing action research on student behavior and response to the lesson, ensuring students have or are using necessary accommodations or RTI interventions</li><li>Performing one-on-one conferencing or task mastery</li><li>Collecting homework, reviewing completion, and assessing student understanding. Use that information to form flexible groups for leveled instruction (re-teaching, enrichment, and catch-up)</li></ul>**Note: The times that a co-teacher is not directly involved with teaching, supporting, or supervising students are to be chosen carefully. 'One teach, one do something else' is not co-teaching if it's the norm.

Co-teacher #1 is	Co-teacher #2 is
Taking attendance	• Leading an antecedent set or review of material taught yesterday
Collecting homework	• Introducing a study skill
Passing out handouts	• Providing directions, modeling the first problem on the assignment, fielding questions about the assignment
Giving instructions orally	• Writing down instructions on the board • Repeating or clarifying difficult concepts • Mind mapping the process. For example, if instructions are to write an essay, provide a graphic organizer framework for that essay on the board.
Parallel teaching with a large mixed-ability or same-ability group of students	• Parallel teaching with a small mixed-ability or same-ability group of students
Parallel teaching: prepping half of the class for one side of a debate	• Parallel teaching: prepping the other half of the class for the opposite side of a debate
Facilitating an independent activity for individualized instruction	• Circulating and checking for comprehension • Implementing accommodations, adaptations, or modifications according to IEP requirements or RTI interventions
Re-teaching or pre-teaching with a small group or half the class	• Monitoring a large group or half the class as they work on an assignment • Facilitating an enrichment activity with a large group or half the class that does not need re-teaching or pre-teaching
Proctoring a test silently with a group of students	• Reading tests aloud to a group of students • Scribing essay answers for specific students • Re-phrasing and clarifying tests questions for a targeted group of students as required by the IEP
Creating lesson plans according to standards, objectives, and curriculum requirements	• Providing suggestions for modifications, accommodations, adaptations, RTI interventions, and differentiating instruction
Facilitating an acceleration center or flexible group	• Facilitating an acceleration center or flexible group
Explaining new content	• Conducting role-play • Modeling a new concept • Asking higher-order thinking questions

Parallel Teaching

Half of class

Same topic

Example: Greek Myths

Each teach half the class the same topic

Half of class

Same topic

Example: Greek Myths

Parallel Teaching

Let's look at parallel teaching. What is it? How do we do it? This approach allows teachers to split the class in half. Group size is smaller, allowing greater supervision by the teacher. While teachers are teaching the same information with this approach, working with a smaller group allows them to identify students who may be having difficulty understanding. In a larger class setting, identifying these students is much more difficult.

Parallel Teaching: Benefits

- Co-planning – Two heads are better than one.
- Allows teachers to work with smaller groups.
- Each teacher has the comfort level of working separately to teach the same lesson.
- Can separate students who feed off each other.

Parallel Teaching: Challenges

- Requires co-planning time.
- Both teachers need to be competent in the content.
- The pace of the lesson must be the same.
- There must be enough flexible space in the classroom.
- The noise level must be controlled.

There are teachers out there - I hope you are not in this situation - who are, literally, teaching classes of 45 students. I've sat in these classrooms as an empathetic coach wracking my brain for solutions to the teacher's daily challenge. Parallel teaching can make the group smaller. Even if you're teaching 20 students, parallel teaching makes the group smaller.

Typically, using a direct-teaching model, when you ask a question, two or three students will answer it. When direct teaching in a parallel teaching model, you ask students a question: If you have fifteen students, three of those fifteen students might answer your question. The other teacher also has fifteen students - three of those students might answer a question. You now have six students participating, and your focus is more closely on those students because they are in close proximity to you because you've divided the class (and space) in half. (Sometimes you might pull that class out into another space if there's a classroom down the hall.) In this model there are twice as many students answering. That's one way to look at it.

Two teachers in the room, both of whom are comfortable with the topic and can teach it equally as well, may teach the same topic; however, though they are teaching the same topic at the same time and covering the same goals, they might teach it a little differently. Consequently, they reach a wider range of learning styles in the classroom.

Another form of parallel teaching may involve dividing the class based on student learning profile; the more hands-on sensory learners are in one group and the verbal-linguistic learners are in the other. You can also minimize behavior problems by separating students who feed off each other.

Logistically, one group of students may be facing a board at the front of the oom and the other group may be facing the side. When they are not writing on the board, the teachers can move into the group a little bit. Proximity to the students allows the teacher to be heard.

One challenge to parallel teaching is that it requires co-planning. If you don't have planning time, you really can't do the parallel teaching model unless – there is one exception – the co-teachers really work well together.

Two math teachers, with whom I once worked, had taught together for years. They would often finish each other's sentences. They had been teaching Algebra I and Algebra II together for four years, so they did not always have to plan together because they both knew the topic really well. Planning for these teachers often consisted of short frequent check-ins and periodic planning.

Both teachers need to be competent in the topic being taught in order for parallel teaching to be a viable option. This model will not work if the special educator part of the math co-teaching team doesn't really know math as well as the general education teacher does (at least enough to teach the specific topic they are teaching together).

You will need space in the classroom to divide the class in half, or a classroom down the hall that you find is empty. Note: This does not mean that every day you parallel teach you should take your group and leave the room. That's not co-teaching. But you may, at times, feel this is the best way to do it.

Noise level must be controlled when parallel teaching. Teachers who find this model successful make a deliberate effort to talk quietly. Interestingly, when teachers model that 'quiet' students follow suit. If you've got two loud teachers, you're going to disturb each other, not to mention distract the students.

Educators often ask, "Does it disturb the students with ADHD in the parallel-teaching environment?" Amazingly, I have not seen that to be the case when the co-teachers keep their voices down. What happens is that, instead of being in front of the whole room as in traditional teaching, when parallel teaching, co-teachers are a lot closer to their students and they speak more softly. That proximity, that closeness, really helps students with ADHD. They actually will function better than when they are way at the back of the room. When in a larger group, students with ADHD and ADD may struggle to focus on the lesson because the teacher is at the front of the room and other things are going on in the room around them and behind the teacher's back.

Alternative Teaching

Large Group

Different topic

Example: Writing Skills

One teach large group & one teach small group

Small Group

Different topic

Example: Basic writing skills focused on accelerating skills

Alternative Teaching

This is another approach that provides for smaller group size.

Alternative teaching provides the option to divide the class into two groups — one advanced, one at class level, or one large and one small — and each group, at any given time, might be taught by each teacher. Then, the students switch teachers.

Interestingly, in one seventh-grade math class where I was coaching, I noticed that the learning strategy specialist was teaching the main class, while the math teacher was at a table with just three students in another part of the room. While debriefing the teachers later, I found that the learning strategy specialist knew the math well enough to conduct the lesson for the whole class. The general education teacher sat with the three students, who really struggled to grasp the concepts, because both teachers felt that the specialist did not strongly grasp the teaching techniques for that concept in math. They agreed that she was not the best one to work with those three students.

© 2010 Susan Fitzell, M. Ed.

When co-teaching, we have to check our ego at the door and make decisions in the best interest of our students. Over the years traditional practice has reinforced the myth that the special education teacher should be with the students that need the basic skills while the general education teacher teaches the whole class. That's not necessarily true. Let the situation dictate the response.

On another occasion, I met a math teacher who was becoming very frustrated. The students with special needs weren't making the necessary gains in math even though the special education teacher had been working with them. It was already March. The math teacher found that the special education teacher knew the math well enough to teach it to the larger group. However, the students who really needed alternate strategies and ways of explaining the math actually got them better from her. Why?

Simple – she's a math teacher and understood the math at a deeper level. In this case, she was able to present the math concept in various ways that the special education teacher didn't necessarily know. Because that was her area of expertise, she could come up with four or five different approaches to teach that concept, whereas the special educator was able to teach it the one way that the teacher's manual presented it. That was fine for the main body of students who were at grade level. However, it didn't work for the ones who were struggling.

The general education teacher had a bigger bag of tricks for teaching the math concepts and a better understanding of the math, so she was the better one to work with the struggling students. She found that as soon as she began implementing intense re-teaching and intervention strategies, her students started advancing in skill levels and in understanding. She had the special education teacher teach the main lesson, so that she could work with the students with special needs and they soon saw better results. This is alternative teaching at its best.

Benefits of Alternative Teaching

- It meets individual needs – both teacher needs and student needs.
- When you're co-planning, two heads are better than one.
- It allows you to work with smaller groups, just like parallel teaching.
- Teachers can be in their comfort level – their own private bubble, whether it's with a certain level of student need, a teaching methodology or a process.
- You can separate students who feed off one another.

Challenges of Alternative Teaching

- Groups must vary or the students in the group will quickly become labeled (e.g., the "smart" group).
- The students might view the teacher working with the larger group as the teacher in control.
- Noise level must be controlled.
- There must be adequate space.

The groups need to vary. If you always have the students with special needs in the same small group, everybody will know, "Oh, those are the sped students." That stigma kills their spirit.

I've seen that slow death of morale and spirit through my years teaching high school. Students would come to me in ninth grade with such low self-esteem, feeling like they were stupid because they had always been in special education classes. When including students in general education classes that are set up for success, teachers have the opportunity to turn that negative message around. When alternative teaching is combined with immediate ongoing assessment as a foundation for forming groups, sometimes students with special needs might actually be in a higher-level group because they understand the topic taught that day!

Consider this example: As teachers, we know that sometimes students with Asperger's – this is also true of autism – really perseverate on a topic. When they are into something, they are all the way into it!

A student was very interested in NASA and space travel. He watched every Discovery Channel program on the solar system and NASA. He read all the books; he had all the action figures; he had accumulated years of knowledge on the topic. In the science class, when we started teaching the solar system he was the expert. He was in the higher level of every activity involving the solar system unit.

The other half of the story is that he usually struggled and was on an Individual Education Plan (IEP). He didn't even have the basic reading skills for his grade level!

This exact situation is addressed in an alternative co-teaching scenario. Students are placed in groups based on their level for any given activity. They might not always be in the lowest-level group. Everyone gets a chance to shine.

Another challenge is that if you always have the special education teacher with the lowest-level students in the smallest group, the students may start viewing the teacher with the small group as the teacher who's not in control. The teacher with the big group is The Teacher - the real teacher and the one in control. Consider the two previous examples: the learning strategies specialist (special education teacher) taught the main lesson with the larger group and the content area specialist (general education teacher) taught the group that was struggling to grasp the concepts.

Alternative Teaching

Half of class	Each teach	Half of class
Different topic	half the	Different topic
Example: Grammar	class, then switch	Example: Poetry

How else could alternative teaching look?

You might have a small group catching up on a missed assignment or completing immediate ongoing assessment. One group might be working with hands-on materials, which other students don't need. The smaller group may be engaged in remedial instruction, or, the smaller group may be engaged in extended challenge work. That small group may consist of students that really are bored and ready to move on. Normally you don't have a chance to do that. Now you can.

Another model for alternative teaching is to divide the class in half. With alternative teaching, co-teachers can capitalize on their teaching strengths and preferences. For example, one teacher may prefer to teach poetry while the other teacher feels very competent teaching grammar. Each teacher can teach half the group skills based on their teaching strengths while students benefit from having multiple teaching styles in the classroom.

In one classroom I observed in Kinston, NC, I saw the best of alternative teaching in action. One teacher was sitting in front of one part of the class. She was a seasoned general education teacher and she was teaching poetry. She absolutely loved poetry and was relishing the opportunity to co-teach. With co-teaching, she was finally able to make room in the schedule to teach poetry and incorporate it into the standards without worrying about teaching grammar. At the same time, the special education teacher – learning strategies specialist – was teaching grammar to the other part of the class. She loved grammar, was good at it, and had many creative ways of teaching it. Not only was she good at grammar, she was good at teaching test-taking skills. The teachers alternated four days a week. They each taught their subject of interest to half the class, every other day, Monday through Thursday.

On Friday they did whole-class activities to make sure they were catching up on and covering all that was necessary to meet the standard requirements of the curriculum. Both were able to teach what they loved, as well as the subject they were most confident and comfortable with. It worked beautifully for the teachers and the students.

Alternative teaching can be useful in schools with economic issues. Suppose there's a shortage of lab equipment. One teacher can be running the lab, while the other one is teaching the content. The next day they switch. Half the class does the lab and half the class learns content. They make do with half the equipment!

In math, one teacher teaches with manipulatives, breaking down the process to make sure students understand it. The other teacher teaches a new concept. The next day they switch.

I observed the following lesson in a co-taught class in Bow, NH: One teacher worked with a group of students to prep one side of a debate in social studies, and the other teacher helped the other half of the class prep their side of the debate. The energy in the room was electric. Students were engaged, challenged, motivated, on-task, and most importantly, learning. Interestingly, they were able to concentrate in spite of the increased noise level. This is not much different from a large dinner party that breaks up into two or three conversations which all go on at once. It worked! How much more difficult this would have been for a single teacher to manage. With two teachers, the lesson went quite smoothly.

Again, when using the alternative teaching approach with one large group and **one small group, it's important that the small group varies. The small group** should not be the lowest achievers on a regular basis. That would be the same as segregating and tracking within the class.

Advanced Co-Teaching: Station Teaching

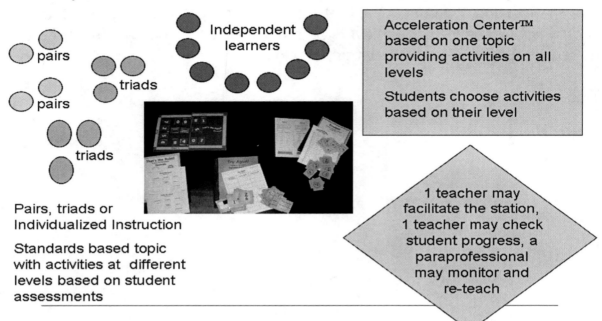

Station Teaching
(Acceleration Center™ Structure)

pairs

pairs

triads

triads

Independent learners

Acceleration Center™ based on one topic providing activities on all levels

Students choose activities based on their level

Pairs, triads or Individualized Instruction

Standards based topic with activities at different levels based on student assessments

1 teacher may facilitate the station, 1 teacher may check student progress, a paraprofessional may monitor and re-teach

The most common model of co-teaching that I encounter is the one teach, one support model. Periodically, I work with teams who have effectively integrated alternative teaching and parallel teaching into their co-teaching methodology. So, one teacher, one support teacher, parallel teaching, and alternative teaching are typically the approaches used in the initial stages of co-teaching. Seasoned co-teachers, who have successfully implemented these models, approach me at almost every seminar I present and ask, "What's the next step? We are looking for advanced co-teaching strategies."

Station Teaching - The Next Step

For the seasoned co-teacher the next step is station teaching. Under that heading there are two advanced co-teaching strategies that are rarely implemented, especially at the secondary level. They are Fitzell Acceleration Centers™ and Flexible Grouping. The benefits of these two models are that they are powerful strategies for:

- Differentiation
- Response to student learning (or non-learning)
- The inclusive classroom

- Multiple ability levels in the classroom
- Student apathy and lack of motivation

Station teaching is an advanced co-teaching structure. It's the next level after one teach, one support, parallel teaching, alternative teaching, and possibly team teaching. It can be combined with any other model. Teachers can divide the class in half as in alternative and parallel teaching, as well as engage students in a Fitzell Acceleration Center or flexible group.

Generically, station teaching may take two forms[1]:

1. There is a "station" in a corner of the room, a piece of the room, a setup in the room, or a crate in the room. Its purpose is to have your students focus on one topic. That topic might be the area in your subject where your students did not do well on the state test last year. That topic might be an aspect of your curriculum that you need to repeat for some students who struggle, or advanced material for those students that need to be challenged beyond the standard curriculum. The goal is to give all your students an opportunity to succeed.

2. Flexible grouping takes the concept of 'station' and considers each group a 'station' in the room, essentially establishing multiple learning 'stations' in the classroom.

Station Teaching Benefits[2]:
- Each teacher has a clear teaching responsibility; both have the opportunity to actively teach.
- Students benefit from individual or small group work.
- Teachers can cover more material more quickly if stations are well-planned and coordinated.
- There are fewer discipline problems when students are engaged in active, hands-on learning appropriate to their ability level. Worksheets and solely verbal linguistic approaches should be kept to a minimum.
- Talkative students can be separated to minimize off-task behavior and classroom disruptions.
- Station teaching maximizes the use of volunteers and extra adults in the classroom because there are always students that need one-on-one or extra support.

---

[1] Station teaching may be described in other resources differently. In this volume, it is presented as an advanced co-teaching strategy clearly differentiated from alternative and parallel teaching models.
[2] Adapted from Partners for Student Achievement: A Co-Teaching Resource Handbook for Cooperating Teachers in VA by the MidValley Consortium for Teacher Education.

Station Teaching Challenges:

- Fitzell Acceleration Centers, as a station teaching method, requires significant one-time preparation.
- Flexible grouping requires ongoing co-planning, assessment and, ideally, tiered lesson plans and activities.
- There may be increased noise in the room, unless teachers consistently teach and enforce the rules of engagement and provide incentives.
- All stations must be paced so teaching ends at the same time or students have options when finished.
- One or more groups must work independently of the teachers.

Fitzell Acceleration Centers™ - A Better Alternative

This model is different from what people visualize when they think of a center. A Fitzell Acceleration Center is not the same as an elementary learning center. It's a combination of several 'station' methods. If you've ever created a learning center or implemented an Accelerated Reading program, or if you are familiar with SRA (Science Research Associates) individualized direct instruction for Reading Mastery, you have worked with different types of stations. The Fitzell Acceleration Center takes the best from each of these models and combines them into a model appropriate at the secondary level.

Note: For the purposes of readability and brevity, all references to "Acceleration Center(s)" in this text are understood to mean "Fitzell Acceleration Center(s)™."

I remember spending an entire week creating a learning center on plants many years ago. Every single night I was cutting out leaves, flowers, and petals. I made hands-on activities using clothespins and construction paper. I spent hours upon hours on this learning center. Friday was the big day. I introduced the center to the students, and explained the instructions. I had that sense of excitement and fulfillment a teacher experiences when having worked so hard to create what they feel should be an award-winning lesson plan. My students finished the center in 45 minutes. All those hours of prep work and it was over in 45 minutes!

Who has the time for that today? My observation is that, generally speaking, teachers do not center-teach anymore. We just don't have the time to prepare learning centers using this paradigm. Additionally, secondary teachers rarely use centers. They may be used in some science classes, but for the most part it's a foreign concept and considered 'elementary'.

Fitzell Acceleration Centers are similar to the concept of a learning center, except that teachers do not create a separate center for every unit they are teaching. They don't have a holiday center, for example, or a math center created for a specific lesson plan. Instead, teachers focus on a curriculum strand taken from the state standard. The activities in the center range from the very basic skills in the strand to the highest level skills and, possibly even college-level material if students can reach that far. That one center or station remains for the entire year, and beyond.

- You make it once and use it all year.
- You prep it once and possibly add to it during the year.
- The only maintenance required is student assessment and re-assignment.

Co-teachers put a tremendous amount of thought into how they will individualize to meet their students' needs, curriculum benchmarks, and state standards. The challenge, and a benefit, of station teaching in the form of Fitzell Acceleration Centers is that it requires significant advanced preparation: once. After you gather the materials, create, and set-up a center, the prep work is done and minimal co-planning is required for the rest of the year.

Despite its challenges, Acceleration Centers are an absolutely wonderful model for advanced co-teaching.

- With a Fitzell Acceleration Center, teachers use standards-based topics and activities aimed at reaching all learning levels.
- Use authentic assessments to determine student learning levels.
- Assess students to identify how they are doing on a daily or weekly basis. Use the data to discover assignments needed in the acceleration center, at all learning levels in the classroom.

You might have students working in pairs or triads, or you might have independent learners. One teacher in a co-taught classroom may facilitate the station while the other teacher might coach a small group or an individual student, teach half the class a mini-lesson, administer one-minute assessments, or perform any number of relevant tasks. The beauty of this model is that, while one teacher is facilitating the station, the other teacher is also engaged in teaching.

A Fitzell Acceleration Center is a designated area, file crate, file drawer, or pocketed bulletin board that provides students with standards-based learning activities, at a range of ability levels, so that students can focus on achieving standards. Acceleration Centers are not more worksheets. They are activities, at varying learning levels, which consider and address student learning styles.

Activities may be hands-on, involve manipulatives, include creativity, or come in the form of investigations or challenges that require critical thinking skills. Ideally, Acceleration Centers incorporate computer-based instruction, often utilizing the one or two computers in the classroom in a way that is impractical with the whole class teaching model. The Acceleration Center may be focused on a particular skill area or on weak areas identified through previous test results.

For example, secondary students are consistently weak in the areas of fractions and measurements. An Acceleration Center may focus completely on fractions and decimals and include activities as basic as matching numeric fractions to a fraction pie or as advanced as the use of decimals in calculus. This fraction / decimal-based Acceleration Center would provide students who are not making adequate yearly progress a forum for accelerating those skills, as well as providing students who are at the highest level of achievement the opportunity to challenge their potential.

Co-teachers choose pockets of time during the week to assign students to work with an Acceleration Center. Students can visit the center to complete activities assigned to them based on current assessment data (for example, exit cards or current curriculum-based measurement). Acceleration Centers provide teachers with a minimum prep solution to vary levels in the classroom. Students are provided time to work, at their ability level, in small groups or independently, to meet standards.

Acceleration Centers are governed by pre-taught and practiced rules and procedures that require students to be responsible and accountable for their own growth. A major advantage of Acceleration Centers is the opportunity to give struggling learners a double dose of academic support, when they're struggling, to grasp a previously taught concept. They provide a forum for presenting information to students in a way that is not necessarily possible with a whole class lesson. Acceleration Centers provide teachers with a format conducive to spending time with students individually or in small groups. It also opens up an opportunity for teachers to do action research, observations of student learning and behavior, or ongoing immediate assessment.

Considering the Benefits of the Fitzell Acceleration Center Model

Every single teacher in the classroom - every adult in the room - has a job. When station teaching, each teacher has a clear responsibility. There's no guesswork, no perception that one teacher is doing everything and the other teacher is not useful.

Students benefit by individual and small group work just as they do with SRA, Accelerated Reader, in learning centers, or with any number of computer programs that promote skill building and acceleration. In each of these situations, students benefit because they are working at or just above their reading level. In addition, when Acceleration Centers are working smoothly, you can actually cover more material faster.

The Fitzell Acceleration Center model allows you to take a certain period of time within the course of a week to focus at the basic level for those students who aren't responding. Those who need intensified instruction in foundational skills are now able to get what they need. Later, they are able to participate during a whole class lesson.

What happens to those students who already understand? While some students are working on the basics, these students can work at a higher grade level on the same topic. Station teaching using Acceleration Centers allows us to reach many different learning levels in our classroom at the same time, effectively and efficiently.

Addressing the Challenges of Implementing Fitzell Acceleration Centers

Prep Time. The biggest challenge teachers face when implementing Fitzell Acceleration Centers is that they require significant one-time preparation. Ideally, teachers can get together during a professional development day, on a summer workshop day, or choose to spend a few days after school to prep a center. Once the prep work is complete, you don't have to do it again and you will have a center that can be used over and over again. You might add to it or adjust it, but you won't have to create a new lesson from scratch.

Keeping students occupied. For Acceleration Centers to work effectively, teachers need to have options for students who finish early. If we try to make sure that students are finishing their assignment at the same time, we will become frustrated with the process. It is simply not possible for all students to finish their center activities at the same time. When a student finishes their goal chart and they've done the things they're supposed to accomplish, have options available for them to choose from.

Wide Range of Abilities. You might have one or more groups of students working independently from the teacher, so if four or five different levels of students are working on different levels of assignments and there are only two adults in the room, you might have some students working on their own. This may or may not be viable in your classroom. Success depends on student behavior, initiative, ability to focus, and student understanding of teacher expectations and related consequences.

Behavior Management. Teachers must have a good handle on discipline and strict rules about how time is managed and how students should behave during Acceleration Center time. Students need to be taught how to behave during this time. Otherwise, and especially if they have never worked with centers before, they might think it's a free-for-all. So we really need to be clear about our expectations and enforce them.

Some teachers struggle with implementing station teaching because of the classroom management challenge the model poses. In reality, when students understand teacher expectations, are given time to practice the rules of engagement, and those rules are enforced while providing incentive for success, teachers actually have fewer discipline problems. Students behave better when they are engaged.

Noise Level. During station teaching, teachers may experience a higher level of noise in the classroom than usual. Decide which students should be partners; ascertain which students will mix best, and put them together deliberately. I may say, "You can work with so-and-so." Or, "I don't want you working with so-and-so." You can separate the talkative students and keep them apart.

The trade-off for a quiet classroom is students who are engaged in the learning process rather than experiencing frustration in their learning. They are doing their work. Since students are being supported by two or three adults in the room, they can actually move up a level.

Fitzell Acceleration Centers Respond to All Learners

The acceleration center approach allows students to work at their ability level. When co-teaching in diverse classrooms with a wide range of ability levels, there are few ways that work better to bridge the gap than station teaching. With acceleration centers, students can work at their ability level in either individualized or small group activities, geared toward accelerating their progress in meeting curriculum goals and state standards.

While students work with activities they have chosen from the Acceleration Center form of station teaching, teachers are free to become facilitators in student learning, as needed. Co-teachers might set up acceleration centers and each monitor one station. For example, one acceleration center might be for writing skills and another for grammar.

If you decide to implement Fitzell Acceleration Centers, start small. Start with one standard and one center with multiple activities at varying levels. I've worked with teachers who get very excited about the concept and immediately start planning three different centers, or a center per teaching unit. I would not advise starting out with more than one center. Start with one. Co-teachers will be less inclined to become overwhelmed with the planning and prep work involved, students have time to practice using centers, and the bugs can be worked out before a new acceleration center is planned.

Fitzell Acceleration Center Flowchart

At a recent workshop that focused on station teaching, one group of teachers created a flowchart that presents the steps to creating an acceleration center in visual format. Credit is due to Ms. Jones, Ms. Johnston, Ms. Tribula, and Ms. Whim who teach at Woodington Middle School in Kinston, NC, for the initial version of this flowchart. The full-color chart, entitled the Fitzell Acceleration Center Concept Map, is available on my website, http://www.SusanFitzell.com. Simply type "acceleration" in the search box on the home page and follow the links.

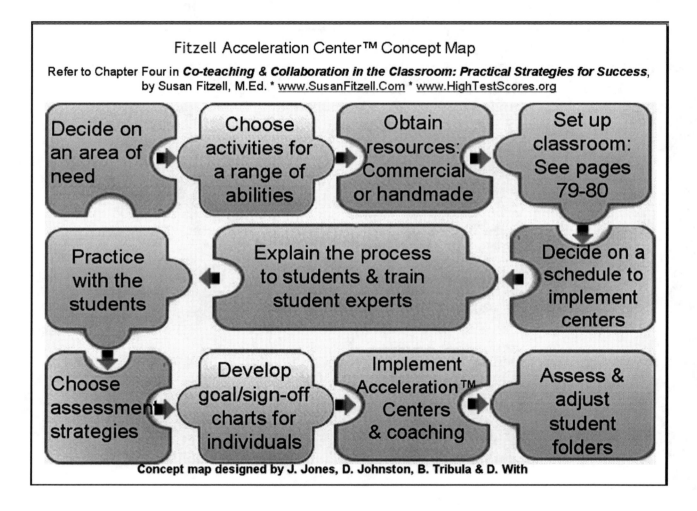

Fitzell Acceleration Center Instructions
Step 1) Decide on Area of Need

The first thing you and your co-teacher must discuss and agree upon is the students' area, or areas, of need and decide where to focus your attention. Let's take a look at some subject-specific areas of need that you and your co-teacher may consider addressing.

If you are co-teaching science, look at your state test scores and determine which questions resulted in the most common student errors. According to the National Assessment of Educational Progress, forty-three percent of American fourth to eighth graders in urban school districts do not have a basic understanding of science. This is a national challenge. Test results may indicate that students cannot read basic charts. We might also have students who can't follow along with simple experiments. If so, we might create a center that focuses on the strands in the science standard that require students to be able to read charts and graphs. We will then add a range of assignments aimed at application of charts and graphs, incorporating following instructions for simple experiments.

In English, students may be struggling with drawing inferences, having trouble with cause and effect, or encountering difficulty with persuasive writing. Examine the standards and look at the strand that includes those concepts. Consider objectives from very basic strands that students might begin to learn in the early grades to skills required three to four years above grade level. Including a wide range of information addresses the needs of advanced students so there is something for everyone in the acceleration center.

In math, most schools I work with are having trouble getting students to pass measurement, fractions, and decimals on their state tests. Using the Fitzell Acceleration Center to provide reinforcement of concepts that are foundational to understanding math is an attractive option. For instance, scheduling station time for this purpose allows opportunities for students to use manipulatives in order to understand fractions. When you are expected to continue moving forward in math, sending students who need reinforcement time to an Acceleration Center for that additional study of basic concepts offers a way for those students to succeed.

For example, I have an acceleration center on fractions and decimals. There are activities in the acceleration center at an appropriate level for those students who can't correctly identify fractions. I may have other students who understand fractions and decimals and therefore need to be challenged to rise to the next level. For those students, I include an activity to figure out the inertia required to get a roller coaster to continue along its path using fractions and decimals.

Fitzell Acceleration Centers include everything from the very basic to the highest level of skill. These activities are *all* in the station, *all* at the same time, and *all* on the same topic. We don't change topics in the acceleration center every month. The center's primary purpose is to focus on one strand in a standard that is critical to student success and to lay a strong foundation for accelerating growth for all learners.

Step 2) Choose Activities for a Range of Abilities

Once we determine our area of need, the next thing to do is come up with a range of activities.

For example, in English, some students could be drawing inferences, some could be working on basic cause and effect, and some students might be learning the basics of persuasive writing. One of the co-teachers can work with a group of students or in a designated section of the room. Students can be separated into pairs or triads with activities at their level taken from the acceleration center.

Other students may already be good at drawing inferences and have high test scores in that area. Suppose they are proficient at persuasive writing. Maybe they can write a nonfiction book or a short story for publication. Perhaps they can create and maintain a blog. Websites like www.edublogs.org offer space for teachers to encourage students to start and maintain a blog as a writing motivator. This type of activity is great for all students, but for the more advanced students, the potential for challenge is an excellent motivator.

Notice that while one teacher is working with one group of students in one section of the room, whether in pairs, triads, or other small groups, the other teacher is working with the rest of the students in another section of the room. All the students are working at their own level on the same strand, or topic, of the curriculum.

In math, you might have students who don't understand the basics of measurement. This will hinder them during full-class lessons when you're trying to get them to build on those skills. They feel that their needs are not being met and begin to fall behind.

The co-teachers in this math class can use the station on measurement and pull out activities for those students that are having difficulty. Even in high school, you can have them measure tables, chairs, and other objects in the room with a ruler or tape measure.

University professors at schools such as the Rochester Institute of Technology report the following phenomenon: Students with high SAT and ACT math scores who have taken Advanced Placement Calculus cannot apply much of it after arriving at engineering school. This is because they've memorized the formulas without really understanding what the math means. We can use the same kind of fun tools for these higher level students: manipulatives, algebra tiles, even Tinker Toys (based on the Pythagorean progressive right triangle[3]) that we use for the students at other levels to help them to develop math models, solve problems, and understand the math. Create an acceleration center that supports math application and short answer items.

A group of teachers had been teaching their students what they called 'power words' for testing: evaluate, compare, contrast, discuss, enumerate, etc. But when the state test results came back, they found that their students' scores were about the same as the previous year.

As a result, they downloaded the previous year's stale test and asked the students to highlight all the words in the test they didn't know. What they realized was that there were many words on the state test which the students didn't know. This group of teachers taught their students what the words meant using a variety of strategies including peer teaching and role-play skits.

One of your Fitzell Acceleration Center activities could be to have copies of previous state test questions for students to review. They can highlight the words they don't know, come up with a creative way to learn those words, and teach those words to another person. While some students are working on vocabulary words from the test, the students that understand the vocabulary and are ready to move on start working on their SAT or ACT vocabulary.

Suppose you want to work on critical thinking skills in multiplication. As a station activity, you might have students listen to Multiplication Rock. One of the best ways for students to learn their multiplication tables is to sing them. This could be a powerful station activity.

---

[3] Strange, Craig. Collector's Guide to Tinker Toys. ISBN 0-89145-703-8.

Students with well-developed critical thinking skills could practice advanced writing by composing a letter to a government official or the author of a favorite novel. This activity could be differentiated for students at varying levels of ability. Experience has shown that when students write to someone they look up to, or about an issue for which they feel strongly, they put more effort into project. When they receive a reply, even if it's a form letter, they are on top of the world.

When teaching science, I would have students pick a cause, then research what bills were before Congress or the State legislature for that cause. I had them research where to write to ask the legislator or representative to act in favor of their cause.

Well, one student chose to write to Mrs. Barbara Bush, the First Lady at that time. I will never forget when he got a letter back. It was near the end of the year - after school - and I heard yelling coming down the hall. My name, "Mrs. Fitzell, Mrs. Fitzell, Mrs. Fitzell!" He burst into the room – a high school student, not a first-grader – absolutely burst into the room and said, "Mrs. Fitzell, I got a letter from Mrs. Bush!" Believe it or not, this student was the biggest behavior problem in my class.

The moral of this story is that by implementing Fitzell Acceleration Centers we are motivating and reaching all levels of learners in the classroom.

Step 3) Obtain Resources, Commercial or Handmade

I don't advocate that teachers stay up all night coming up with ideas, lesson plans, and materials for centers. Instead, I'll show you where you can purchase or get free materials for your centers. We don't have to reinvent the wheel, or create everything from scratch. There are materials on the market that are perfect for Fitzell Acceleration Center activities.

For example, Walch Publishing offers a product series for middle schools called *Building Math*. This three-book series uses hands-on investigations and group activities to excite and engage students in learning algebra and data analysis. The books, *Everest Trek, Stranded!* and *Amazon Mission* (for grades 6-8) guide students through simulations of climbing the world's tallest mountain, being marooned on a desert island, and navigating a mighty river basin. Students face one math challenge after another, continually building skills.

Another ready-made product that slips beautifully into Acceleration Centers is The Math Learning Center's *Math and the Mind's Eye* series (www.mathlearningcenter.org). For example, in Unit IX: Picturing Algebra, students explore formulae, algebraic notation, equivalent expressions, and equations using toothpicks and algebra manipulatives. The centers are done for you; it's a hands-on way to teach an understanding of algebra and pre-algebra.

Evan-Moor Educational Publishers (www.evan-moor.com/centers) offers hands-on materials, through grade seven, for many of the strands we teach. Their center activities are called "Take it to Your Seat" centers. The center looks like a workbook; you open it up, tear out the pages, cut out and laminate the pieces and you have a center! Though they're not free, they are inexpensive. This product is one I've used in my Fitzell Acceleration Center.

Also, www.HandsonEnglish.com has activities to make English hands-on. Although it's a website for ESL students, there are some excellent strategies for English center activities. There is a nominal subscription fee for this service.

One of the best ways to get free solutions and free activities is to do a Google search for the topic and lesson plans. For example, if you want to find hands-on lesson plans about drawing inferences, your Google search would be, "drawing inferences" "lesson plans" "hands-on". Take special note of search results that say "Elementary", as these items often contain center ideas that can be adapted to the secondary classroom. This may take some time, but it's free. Another great way to find free materials is to Google websites geared to home-schoolers. Home-schooling websites have many lesson plans and activities, often free of charge. These sites also have an abundance of hands-on lesson plans.

Step 4) Arrange Your Classroom Environment for Success

Once you have identified your students' needs, settled on a center topic, and chosen a variety of appropriate activities, it's time to set up the classroom!

NOTE: All the remaining steps apply to both types of station teaching: Fitzell Acceleration Centers and flexible grouping. Flexible Groups Classroom Options 2 and 3 (below) also work well for parallel and alternative teaching.

One day, while coaching at a middle school in North Carolina, I entered a small classroom and found that the co-teachers had divided the class in half and were doing alternative teaching. They had arranged the desks in a conference table style. The two teachers were at either end, so as not to drown each other out. Because it was like a conference table with the students so close together and the teacher right there, they had complete behavioral control. It was one of the most effective uses of small space I've ever seen.

Develop a Class Plan for Differentiating Within Groups

- Decide on a physical classroom desk and table arrangement.
- Will one room arrangement work or will teachers need to have options for multiple arrangements depending on the group activity required?
- How will the class be rearranged when necessary? What will be required to accomplish rearranging the classroom?
- What routines and skills are necessary for students to learn to have the class run smoothly when we deviate from the traditional row arrangement? Have students practice moving from one room arrangement to another.
- Use a signal, either a hand gesture or a sound, to notify students of time remaining until a transition, then use the signal again when the transition needs to occur. Before any transition, remind students of behavioral expectations.

The goal in designing the classroom to be conducive to small group work is to design a structure that allows the teacher or co-teachers to interact quickly and easily with all students.

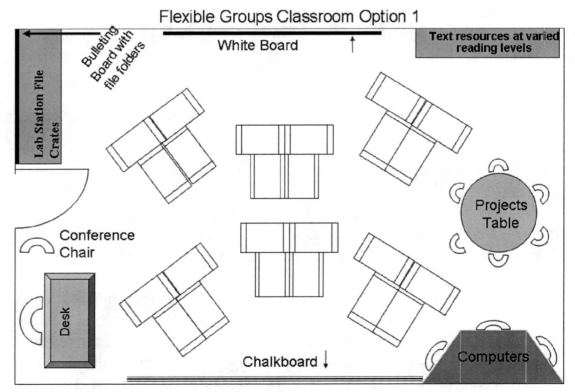

Flexible Groups Classroom Option 1

24 Students – Groups of 4 + small group option for projects & computer work

Flexible Groups Classroom Option 2

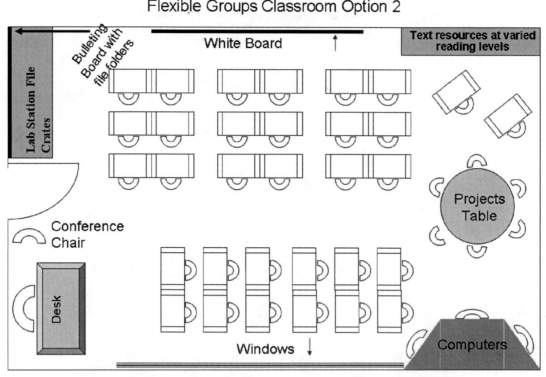

32 Students- Pairs & Divided Class w/ small group options

Flexible Groups Classroom Option 3

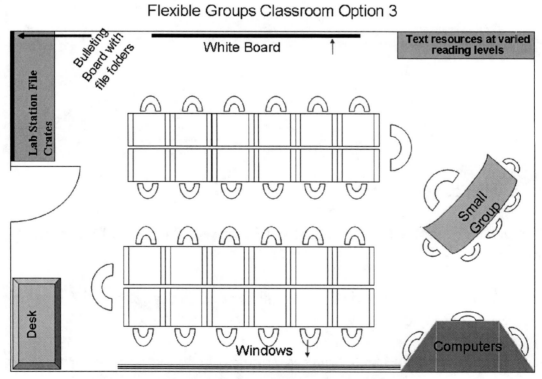

29 Students- Divided Class w/ small group options

Classroom Planning Worksheet

Use this space to sketch out your classroom arrangement ideas

Things to think about:

Will this arrangement work for all activities or will it need to be rearranged for certain things?

If rearrangement will be needed, how will that be accomplished? Can the students do it quickly and safely?

Will co-teachers be able to clearly see each other in order to coordinate activities and communicate?

Step 5) Decide on a Schedule to Implement Centers

Teachers have so much material to cover that it's unlikely you can use Acceleration Centers every day. Most teachers don't. Some will cover curriculum material during the first four days of the week and do stations on Friday. Others may do stations two periods a week. Some co-teachers can divide the period in half and alternate groups.

As a co-teaching team, discuss your goals and your schedule and then stick to what you agree on. Implement centers according to your schedule. Start small and grow with your success.

Step 6) Train Student Experts

Suppose I have ten minutes to focus on coaching. I want that time to be uninterrupted. The last thing in the world I want during a coaching session is to be bombarded by students asking, "What do I do next, Mrs. Fitzell?" "Now what do I do, Mrs. Fitzell?" "Mrs. Fitzell, will you check this for me?"

A significant benefit to station teaching is having the time to work closely with students one-on-one or in small groups. Keeping that benefit in the face of interruptions requires that we spend time at the beginning of the process teaching students how to use centers and training student experts who can help you manage your centers.

These students aren't experts on the content. They are experts on how the station works, how to check activities in and out (including inventorying materials), and what to do after completing an activity. What do you do next? And so on.

The student expert is trained to answer questions like, "I don't understand what the teacher wants me to do." "Who is my partner supposed to be?" "What do I do next?" "What do I do if I'm finished?" so that students in centers do not need to interrupt the teacher.

You might even consider training your biggest, baddest, most difficult student to be your expert because that student is going to think, "Oh, I'm an expert!" I have seen some of the most difficult-to-manage ADHD students become the most amazing peer leaders when given the opportunity. You'll be amazed how well this approach can work.

Step 7) Practice with the Students

Practice behavioral expectations for the station teaching model. Students know how to do a worksheet, they know how to pretend they're following along, but they don't necessarily know how to get out of their seat, go sit with a partner, get to work, and stay on task without disrupting other students along the way. We have to teach them these skills.

I've been asked, "How can I make centers work in a 45-minute class period? There isn't enough time." My first answer is always to use timers. As teachers today, we need to be very efficient with our use of time. Teach students how to move in the classroom, from one activity or station to another, quickly and quietly. Train them. Make it a contest or a game and reward them for transitioning between activities very quickly.

I have seen middle school classrooms with gifted students, ADHD students, students with Asperger's syndrome, and even students with Tourette's syndrome successfully manage these movement challenges. The teachers in these classrooms have drilled the students to practice how to move the desks and regroup. The students are successful. They do it silently, they move quickly, and they finish within 15 to 20 seconds. Seconds! I've been in awe at that.

The teachers make it a contest. They train their students to meet the expectations and periodically give incentives; "Gosh, you guys did so well today when moving into groups that I'm going to give you..." some incentive. The students just love it.

In high school, teachers will say, "All right, the whole class transitioned into groups in ten seconds. None of my other classes have done it that fast." Then, in the next class, the teacher says, "Hey, my last class did it in ten seconds – do you think you can beat them?" Students love to meet that challenge and earn bragging rights for their class. This stuff is straight out of Dale Carnegie, but so what? It works!

Step 8) Choose Assessment Strategies

When thinking about how to assess students in stations, consider assessment strategies you are already familiar with like accelerated reader, SRA, one-minute assessments, or the kind of short tests you might adapt from a workbook.

To ensure the fidelity of an assessment, have a pre-test and a post-test before students move to the next level. This quick check can be done by the co-teacher.

When the learning strategy specialist is performing assessments, they will need the teacher's manual and the answer key.

I was working with several co-teaching teams and one teacher approached me to complain that, sometimes, her math co-teacher gave students the wrong answer or told them how to do something incorrectly. That teacher's credibility suffered when students realized she had given them erroneous information. I asked the teacher, "Does your co-teacher have an answer key?" She said, "No." Our co-teachers need the manual and the answer key in order to effectively support student process and learning. I know that sounds like a revolutionary idea, but if we want our collaborative partners to be able to help students, they need to have the materials to do it well.

On-the-spot assessment techniques that check for understanding:
- Zero-, three-, five-finger response (see visual representation below).
- Use white board responses to assess.
- Exit cards (also known as 'tickets to leave')

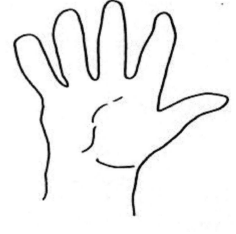

I know nothing about the topic

I know a little bit

I know a lot about this and I'd love to share what I know with the class!

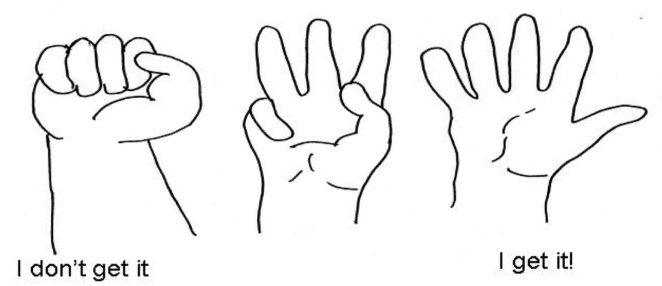

I don't get it

I get it for the most part, but still have some questions

I get it!

Use white boards to encourage participation and for assessment

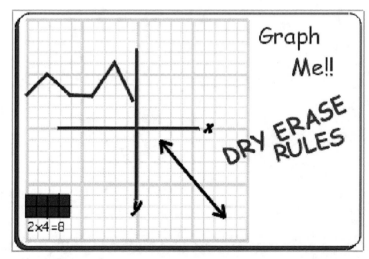

Every student has a white board. Use dry-erase marker or wipe-off crayon. An old child-sized sock serves as eraser and storage of markers.

The teacher asks a question and students write their answers on the white boards.

After a fair amount of time, the teacher asks students to hold up their boards.

The teacher can see how ALL students are doing with one look around the room.

This strategy eliminates blurters and allows those who need processing time to finally get it!

Exit cards

The use of exit cards is a simple assessment tool. Each card will have a set of just two or three questions for students to answer after you teach a lesson. Students answer the questions before the bell rings. It's the last thing they do in class. They must hand it to the teacher before they walk out the door, hence the name "exit cards."

At the elementary level they hand it to the teacher before they move on to the next assignment or the next activity. It's ongoing, immediate assessment in action. If you have two teachers, you have two people who can assess and group the exit cards. Using the results of this assessment, you can determine groups based on criteria that would best support the goals of the small group activity or Acceleration Center. Exit cards (a.k.a. "tickets to leave") are used to gather information on student readiness levels, understanding of concepts just taught, interests, and/or learning profiles.

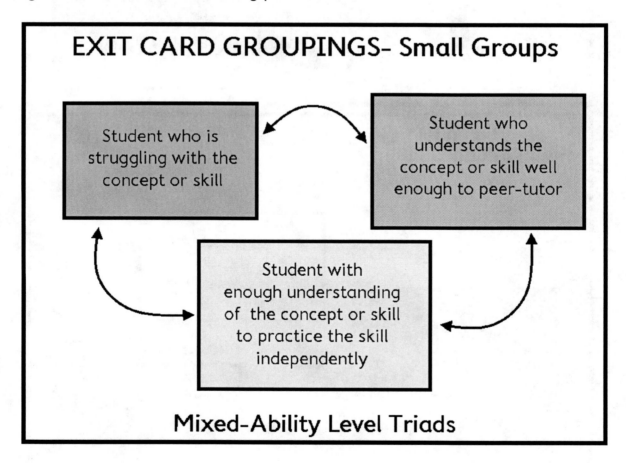

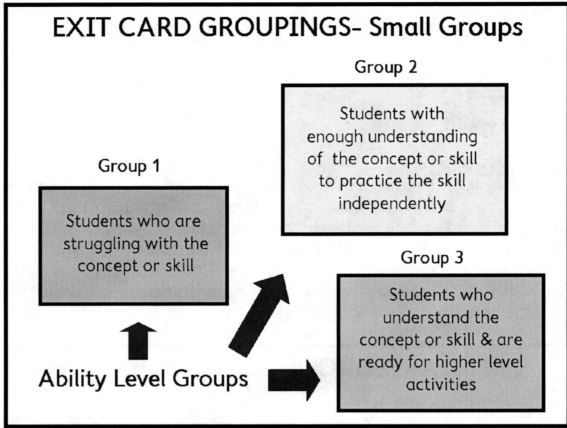

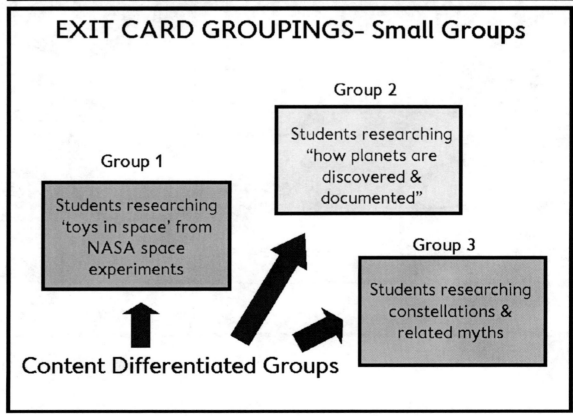

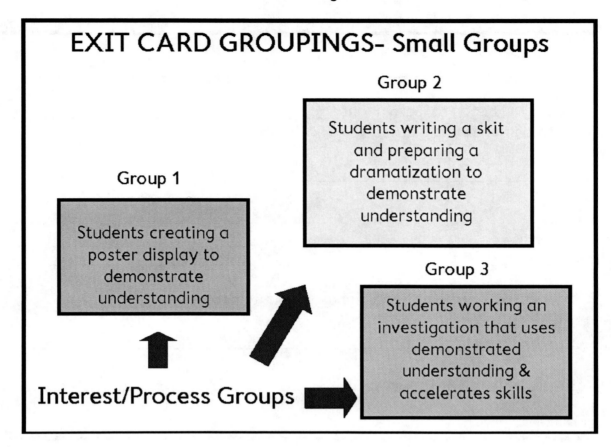

Name: _____ Date: _____

Today, you began to learn about _____:
List three things you learned:

1._____

2._____

3._____

Write at least one question you have about this topic.

_____

_____

_____

Name: _____ Date: _____

Today, you began to learn about _____

What area gave you the most difficulty today?

_____

_____

Something that helped me in my learning today was:

_____

_____

_____

Name: _____ Date: _____

Explain the difference between _____ and

_____. Give some examples of each as part of your explanation.

_____

_____

_____

_____

_____

Name: _____ Date: _____

We used the following learning strategies in this lesson:

1. _____

2. _____

3. _____

What learning strategy or strategies seemed to work best for you?

_____

_____

_____

Step 9) Use Goal Charts to Manage Accelerated Learning

This is a critical step in the implementation of Fitzell Acceleration Centers. Goal Charts (illustrated in the Acceleration Center Components section) are used for each assignment to manage student learning, for individualization, and for acceleration.

Again, this is *critical*! Every student must have a goal chart. This aspect of acceleration centers takes pre-planning. You may want to review the goal charts weekly or once every two weeks. The timing of your reviews depends on two things: how much time you will spend working with the Acceleration Centers, and how quickly students finish their goal sheets.

Step 10) Implement Acceleration Centers & Coaching

Try an application of your chosen model. Start small. Take baby steps towards implementation. If it's overwhelming, you are probably trying to do too much all at once.

Brett and Kate, a co-teaching pair from Penacook, NH decided to do just that; try it. They chose one standard strand: mastering multiples, multiplication, and division. Then they set up one center with four stations around the room to practice the strand at different levels. Each center presented a challenge activity using a different game format.

In a debrief session afterwards, Kate said, "Not only did all the students in the class increase their proficiency on the standard, we had an unexpected surprise. One of our students has been numb to school all year. No matter what we did, we could not motivate him. After we introduced the acceleration center, he was so excited that he kept asking when we could do it again. We were amazed at his enthusiasm and his assessment showed improvement. The acceleration center activity worked."

Brett and Kate started with one concept: multiplication. After implementation, they were happy with the results. Now they can add to the foundation, incorporating more activities at different levels for skills in the math strand for multiplication.

Step 11) Assess and Adjust Student Folders

- Does it work? If so, great!
- Does it need improvement? If it does, make the necessary adjustments.
- Does the data indicate negative gains? If so, discard it and try something else.

Acceleration Center Components

Individualized student goal charts: Goal charts are divided into three sections: required, optional, and choose one, two, or three. There are two chart levels; one for self-starters and one for students who need more support. Charts for students who need more support, especially reading support, might include illustrations, have additional required components, and have fewer optional activities. Do not reduce choices for students who need more support, because choices are motivational. (Goal Chart Symbols: LS = Learning Support, IL = Independent Learner.)

Coaching session: Teacher conferencing or teacher-led small group. Coaching sessions offer teachers the opportunity to lead individuals or small groups of students in assignments appropriate to their achievement level.

Written response journals: This component allows students the opportunity to practice written response skills required to meet state standards and written response goals for math, English, language arts, social studies, or science.

Independent reading or study: This option provides students with the opportunity to improve reading skills and/or provides time to study. (Vocabulary words, flash cards, etc.) If this option is used for study, students should use strategies based on their learning style. It would be a waste of Acceleration Center time to have students study ineffectively. Avoid having students study by completing worksheets, staring at their books, writing things three times each, or using any number of ineffective strategies that students typically use to fail. Students who are working on reading skills should be using materials at, or just slightly above, their reading level. *It is imperative that teachers know the readability levels of the texts students are reading.*

Acceleration Center Folder

Acceleration Goal & Sign-Off Chart

Coaching Session Notes

List of Unit Vocab Words

Flash Cards

Written Response Journal

Acceleration component: Assignment in this component is targeted to address student difficulties and accelerate student learning.

1. Color Coded Folders

2. Labeled Categories

3. Inventory all materials for each activity in folders

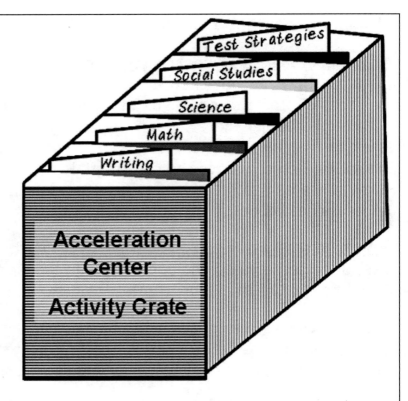

Acceleration Center Crate Conceptualized by Powell & Striker

Keep Inventory

Recently I was doing a full-day workshop on Fitzell Acceleration Centers, and a teacher who had been doing learning centers for many years was in the group. She said, "You forgot a piece. You must have an inventory sheet. Have students doing inventory with a checklist, or you're going to be missing parts the next time students go to do the activity."

Inventory all materials, and teach your student experts to check the inventory after each session. It may be a small step, but it's an important one!

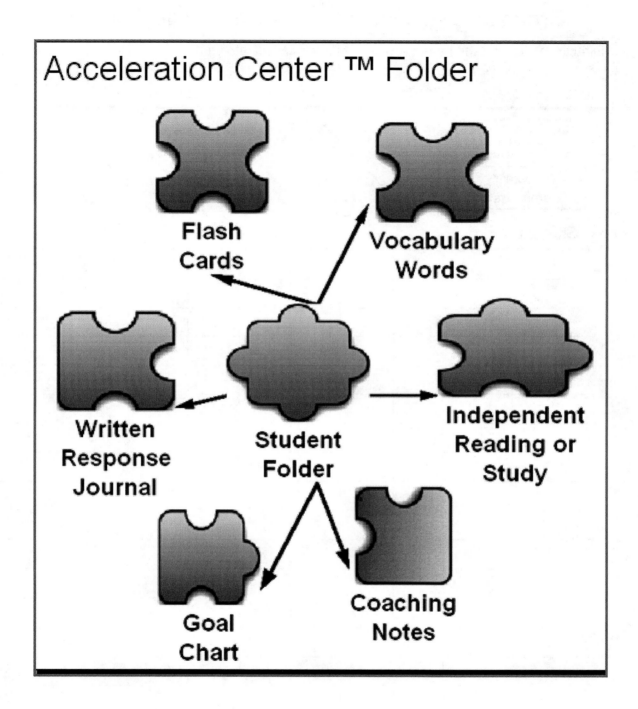

Group Process Observation – Data Collection Chart

Directions: List skills to be observed on slanted lines. Rate student success on a scale of 1-5.

Date: **Subject:**   **Section:**

Scale: 1-5
1= Not observed
5= Consistently Demonstrated

Student Name						Notes

Acceleration Center Goal Chart & Sign-off

Name_____ Date_____

Coaching Group Name_____

Have-To's		Mon	Tue	Wed	Thu	Fri
Coaching Session						
Written Response Journal						
Test Prep (Flash cards, peer practice, etc.)						
Acceleration Component						

Once-a-Weekers	Mon	Tue	Wed	Thu	Fri
Challenge Activity or Investigation					
Independent Reading or Study					

Choices (Examples)	Mon	Tue	Wed	Thu	Fri
United Streaming Video on topic					
Flashcardexchange.com or Quia.com					
Accelerated Reader					
Independent Reading on Topic					

Multi-day Chart - LS

Acceleration Center Goal Chart & Sign-off

Name_____ Date_____

Coaching Group Name_ _____

Have-To's	Mon	Tue	Wed	Thu	Fri
Coaching Session					
Written Response Journal					
Acceleration Component					

Once-a-Weekers	Mon	Tue	Wed	Thu	Fri
Challenge Activity or Investigation					
Independent Reading or Study					
Test Prep (Flash cards, peer practice, Design-A-Test, etc.)					

Choices (Examples)	Mon	Tue	Wed	Thu	Fri
United Streaming Video on topic					
Flashcardexchange.com or Quia.com					
Accelerated Reader					
Peer Tutoring					

Multi-day Chart - IL

Acceleration Center Goal Chart & Sign-off

Name_____ Date_____

Coaching Group Name_____

Weekly Have-To's	Sign-off
Coaching Session (10 min)	
Written Response Journal (10 min)	
Acceleration Component (10 min)	

Choices (10 min) (Examples)	Sign-Off
United Streaming Video on topic	
Flashcardexchange.com or Quia.com	
Challenge Activity or Investigation	
Independent Reading on Topic	
Test Prep (Flash cards, peer practice, etc.)	

Comments & Notes:

Once-a-Week Chart - LS

Acceleration Center Goal Chart & Sign-off

Name_____ Date_____

Coaching Group Name_____

Weekly Have-To's	Sign-off
Coaching Session (10 min)	
Acceleration Component (10 min)	

Choices (10 min) (Examples)	Sign-Off
United Streaming Video on topic	
Flashcardexchange.com or Quia.com	
Challenge Activity or Investigation	
Independent Reading on Topic	
Test Prep (Flash cards, peer practice, etc.)	
Written Response Journal (10 min)	

Comments & Notes:

Once-a-Week Chart – IL

Acceleration Center Goal Chart & Sign-off

Name_____ Date_____

Coaching Group Name_____

Have-To's		Mon	Tue	Wed	Thu	Fri
Coaching Session						
Written Response Journal						
Test Prep (Flash cards, peer practice, etc.)						
Acceleration Component						

Once-a-Weekers	Mon	Tue	Wed	Thu	Fri

Choices (Examples)	Mon	Tue	Wed	Thu	Fri

Multi-day Chart - LS

Acceleration Center Goal Chart & Sign-off

Name_____ Date_____

Coaching Group Name_ _____

Have-To's	Mon	Tue	Wed	Thu	Fri
Coaching Session					
Written Response Journal					
Acceleration Component					

Once-a-Weekers	Mon	Tue	Wed	Thu	Fri

Choices (Examples)	Mon	Tue	Wed	Thu	Fri

Multi-day Chart - IL

Acceleration Center Goal Chart & Sign-off

Name_____ Date_____

Coaching Group Name_____

Weekly Have-To's	Sign-off
Coaching Session (10 min)	
Written Response Journal (10 min)	
Acceleration Component (10 min)	

Choices (10 min) (Examples)	Sign-Off

Comments & Notes:

Once-a-Week Chart - LS

Acceleration Center Goal Chart & Sign-off

Name_____ Date_____

Coaching Group Name_____

Weekly Have-To's	Sign-off
Coaching Session (10 min)	
Acceleration Component (10 min)	

Choices (10 min) (Examples)	Sign-Off

Comments & Notes:

Once-a-Week Chart – IL

Group Processing: How Did We Do?

On a scale of 1-7 rate your group performance:	1	2	3	4	5	6	7
Stayed on task							
Respectful listening							
Encouraging each other							
Starting on Time							
Coming to the session prepared							

Summarize progress made during this small group session

Tips for Successful Acceleration Centers

- Reassign partners every four to five weeks.

- Don't change partners in response to student requests or complaints. Doing so opens up a Pandora's box of potential problems.

- Acceleration Center assignments must be able to be managed and completed independently. If students cannot manage the assignments by themselves they will often stop completely or interrupt the teachers and/or other small groups for help. The goal of the center is for students to be able to increase achievement but also for teachers to gain valuable conferencing time or small group work time uninterrupted. Teachers must be able to optimize Acceleration Center time.

- Acceleration Centers are not thematic nor do they become obsolete at any point during school year. Avoid any seasonal connotation. They are set up for sustainability, requiring minimal prep work when prep for the centers is viewed in light of creating lesson plans suitable for an entire school year.

- Use Acceleration Centers to support state standards or curriculum goals from basic to proficient.

- Create procedures and rules for utilizing the Acceleration Centers with students as part of the process. By doing so, teachers engage students in the process they are more likely to buy into.

- If setting up more than one center, start with the first one and practice the rules and procedures using the first one as a teaching tool.

- As silly as it may sound to a secondary teacher, whether middle school, junior high, or high school, it is imperative to have students practice moving from their seats to the Acceleration Center to choose an activity and back to their seats or small groups until they can do it quietly and efficiently. This typically will take 10 or 15 minutes of practice, set up as a timed contest. Use a stopwatch and practice until students can run the procedure in three minutes or less. It may be beneficial to incorporate a reward system to maintain proper behavior and efficiency over the course of the school year.

- Keep records of completed assignments and how those assignments align to state standards or curriculum goals.

- Train one or two "student experts" on how the Acceleration Centers function. They do not need to know how to do the academic portion of the center; rather, they need to teach other students how to follow the instructions in the folders, how to keep the center organized, and how to explain the logistics of the center to other students. The "student expert" makes it possible for students to work without interrupting the teacher while the teacher is coaching others.

Station Teaching
(Flexible Group Structure)

1 enrichment group, 1 "on-track" group and
1 review group, etc.

Or, three mixed ability groups with
differentiation by process: 1 hands-on
activity, 1 computer based activity, 1 oral or
dramatic activity

Or Multiple groups with teachers circulating

Each teacher
facilitates one group, a
third group may run
independently or with a
paraprofessional

Flexible Grouping

Having certain students in the same groups all the time never allows those
students to move out of the group or up in learning level. A good example of
this is the old reading group idea. Students would be assigned to the blue bird
group, the green bird group, or the red bird group for their reading lessons. The
reason the reading group methodology didn't work is because students stayed
at the same level and proceeded at the same pace all the time. By using exit
cards to continually assess growth and knowledge, teachers can have students
advance levels much more quickly. They may be at a lower level during one
assignment, but in another assignment they may be at a higher level, depending
on the skills required and the student's strengths and weaknesses.

In a co-teaching environment, I group students by assessment results. We do
exit cards as students leave the class. After class, or during prep time,
preferably with my co-teacher, we divide the cards into three groups by ability
levels. The next day, we place students at the ability level they achieved on the
concept they learned the day before. We know what needs reinforcement and
we know which students need to move on. This process addresses the question
of how to meet the different needs of students at different levels in the same
classroom.

Co-teaching Might Look Like This:

- One co-teacher works with a group of students who are struggling with a concept or skill.
- The other co-teacher works with students who understand the skill and are ready to move to the next level.
- A third group of students might be working by themselves, practicing the skill.

Grouping Flexibly with Triads

- One student who has struggled with the concept
- One student who understands the concept well enough to peer tutor
- One student who has some understanding of the concept but isn't yet proficient

This will give you a room full of groups of three, each with a student who knows the topic well enough to peer tutor. Don't use any one model all the time, because students who are constantly used as tutors eventually resent it. It's a good experience for them as long as it's not all the time.

When co-teaching, one teacher can be circulating, observing, and even collecting data on the triads while the other teacher is focused on a coaching session. If Johnny, Jane, and Jimmy didn't get the concept at all yesterday, one teacher can re-teach to them while the rest of the class works in triads.

You might also set up three stations, with one station that allows students to work independently. Stations allow co-teachers to have one group working on advanced material while another group works on targeted interventions designed to accelerate learning and bridge gaps in understanding. A third group would be working independently during this time.

Co-teaching can supercharge station teaching and allow us to do much more to meet different learning levels when teaching this way. It could be the simple one teach, one support model or, for an even broader reach and with the investment of some planning time, flexible grouping and co-teaching can be a dynamic combination.

Here are some examples:

1) Flexible grouping is the most commonly referenced form of station teaching when researching co-teaching models. Exit cards work beautifully for flexible grouping. For instance, if I'm doing flexible grouping, I might have one enrichment group, one on- track group, and one review group. I could have

each teacher facilitate one of the two groups and one group working on its own.

2) You might also have three mixed-ability groups differentiated by process. For example, one group of students engages in a hands-on activity to learn the planets. Another group of students uses a computer-based activity to determine how far apart planets are from one another. The third group creates a dramatic skit to teach the rest of the class about the solar system and the planets. This type of flexible grouping is 'differentiating by process.'

3) Another model of flexible grouping has each mixed-ability group working on the same concept and output requirements. However, each group may vary on how they collaborate to accomplish that assignment. In this model, teachers circulate amongst the groups supporting students as needed. Another option: one teacher supervises and supports while the other teacher collects data.

Small Groups and Flexible Grouping Basics

For teachers who are most comfortable with direct teaching via whole-class teaching, moving toward small groups and flexible grouping can be very intimidating. This is especially true in situations where group dynamics in the classroom are extra-lively and teachers are concerned about managing behavior and keeping kids on task. This section provides strategies and techniques for effectively implementing small groups and flexible groups.

What Constitutes Effective Small-Group Construction?

Effective small-group instruction:
- Uses assessment data to create lesson plans and determine the groups.
- Keeps groups small, preferably three to four students to a group. Sometimes it might even be appropriate to have pairs.
- Groups are flexible. This means that groups change as students grow, test out of a curriculum section, choose activities based on the type of activity required, etc.
- Learning profile instructional materials are geared toward student ability levels when activities are not based on differentiating by process or student.
- Small-group activities are tailored to address student needs.

Ineffective small-group instruction:
- Has kids in groups, but all activity is directed by the teacher.
- Keeps kids in the same groups continually, usually in same-ability groups. This is actually tracking within a class.

- Uses the same materials with all students in all groups.
- Uses the same independent-state work assignments for the entire class.
- Uses small groups to complete worksheets, and more worksheets, and more worksheets.

Grouping arrangements

Teacher directed:

- Small group
- Same-ability
- Mixed-ability
- One-to-one (this is usually an option for our one-to-one conference teacher)

Student directed:

- Acceleration Centers
- Peer tutoring, think-pair-share, drill and practice
- Cooperative learning
- Independent work with the option of having students support each other when necessary
- Triads: one high achiever, one mid-range achiever, one low achiever

Pairs:

- Partners with different learning styles
- One high achiever with one low achiever (but not the lowest)
- Ability-based pair

Some Effective Flexible Grouping Options

- Students might be grouped by readiness, interest in the topic or a learning process, or their student learning profile.
- Students might be grouped by student similarities or dissimilarities, ability levels or same ability levels, using strategic behavioral grouping, self-starters with students who need support to get started, etc.
- Students might be grouped by the teacher planning the group, by students choosing their partners, or through random group generation.

If you were a fly on the wall in a classroom that is fully engaged in flexible grouping, you might see small groups of the same ability working together, mixed-ability groups, pairs and partners, and even some one-on-one interaction.

Types of Groups

- An ability group is a group where all the students are at the same level.

- A mixed-ability group includes students of all different levels together, strategically placed.
- A flexible group is one which will have different members at different times. That, by the way, is the main goal. Students don't get pigeonholed or typecast this way.

When I am ability-grouping with exit cards, using curriculum-based measurement, or grouping on a weekly basis, I can practice flexible grouping.

Options for Determining Which Students Should Be in Which Groups

There are several methods teachers can use to form groups. One way is to use assessment data to group kids. For example, teachers might use standardized test scores, curriculum-based measurement, progress monitoring, or informal assessments such as classroom observations, exit cards, action research, observation, and student self-assessment.

Group students based on targeted areas of instruction. If students did poorly on a specific state standard or are struggling to understand a curriculum concept, those students might be grouped together to accelerate growth.

Students might also be grouped in mixed-ability groups so that in every group there are peer tutors and supports in place for students who are struggling. Sometimes we may simply want pairs. The diagram below demonstrates how you might form pairs. Sort your class roster by grades, then divide the class in half and pair students as illustrated. This process ensures that you never pair the highest student with the lowest and provides different pairs each week, based on student averages.

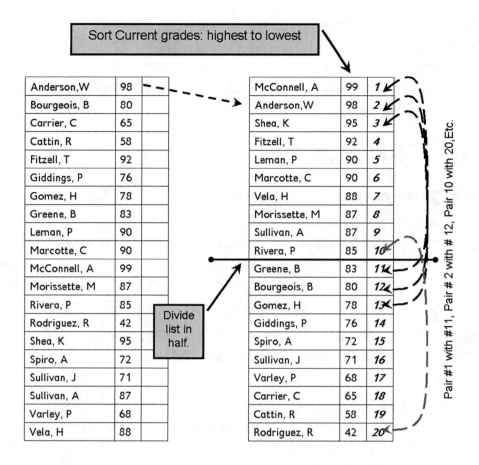

Options for Implementing Ongoing Assessment in a Classroom to Define Groups

Use student data sources as a guide for grouping students. Some sources include:

- A student's journal entries
- Short-answer test responses
- Open-response test results
- Homework completion
- Notebook checks
- Class participation
- Previously completed projects
- Problem-solving skills

Teacher-generated data:

- Anecdotal records
- Teacher observation
- Class discussion
- Rubrics
- Exit cards
- Individualized assessment

- Student-teacher conferencing
- Observation of small group interaction
- Data collected during class discussion (one teacher leads discussion while the other teacher takes notes on student responses and behavior)

Strategies for Effective Group Processes

Establish ground rules. In order for students to behave appropriately and stay on task during small group work, they have to be taught how to work in a group. Students have been trained over the years to sit at desks lined up in rows and passively receive information. Many, if not most, students have no idea how to work in a group. If they have experience with group work it might be quite limited because schools still teach primarily through a direct teaching, whole-class model. So when students are suddenly asked to work in a group, they often misbehave and mismanage their time. They simply don't know how to do small group work.

Consequently, teachers need to teach students how to work in a group. The first step in the process is to establish ground rules and norms for interaction. These are the guidelines that must be enforced by teachers and students themselves in order for group work to be effective. Ground rules should encourage positive collaborative behaviors amongst all students. In my experience, students abide by rules best when they have a part in making them. Guidelines/ground rules need to be posted in the classroom so students can readily refer to them. If students or teachers believe that additional rules are needed, they can be added later.

A very effective technique for teaching students appropriate small group behavior is to have students take an active role in identifying what appropriate behavior actually looks like. It's worth taking the time to do some role-play with the students to show the difference between an ineffective group and an effective group. Another very effective strategy is to have students give their input on inappropriate behavior – for example, putting other students down in the group or laughing at group members' ideas. Students are more likely to comply if they have agreed with reasonable behavior and consequences.

Here are some suggested ground rules:
- Start on time.
- Practice respect for yourself and others.
- Come prepared to do your part.
- Be a good listener.
- No putdowns.
- Make sure everyone gets a chance to contribute or speak.

- Accept constructive criticism gracefully.
- Critique ideas, not people.
- Stay on task.
- No interruptions; let people finish talking.
- Ask for help when you're confused about what to do.
- Help others when you can.
- Do your fair share of the work.

Establish Teacher Expectations for Small-Group Work

- Describe, show an example, or model the expectations for assignments and activities.
- Provide models and examples of what the outcome should, and should not, look like.
- Rehearse the expectations.
- Notice positive group behavior.
- Correct misbehavior and teach appropriate behavior and expectations (we cannot assume that students know what to do).
- Review expectations frequently.

Introducing the Group Activity

- Arrange tasks so all students are within the teacher's view.
- Be thorough when explaining instructions and giving directions.
- Make sure students understand what they are going to do and why they are going to do it.
- Be clear in stating teacher expectations.
- Establish time limits and provide checkpoints within those time limits. For example, if students are going to work in small groups for 15 minutes, check in with students as a whole class to make sure they are on track every three to four minutes.
- Describe and model the final product.
- Monitor small groups and provide guidance as needed.

Reflection Notes

Grading Small Group Work

A common complaint from parents, students, and some teachers about small group work is: "One or two students do all the work while the other students are slackers." This issue is a valid complaint when teachers grade the small group with one grade for the whole group. There are other options. Below is one way to grade small group work:

# Points Possible	Item Graded
This is an individual grade.	Each student in the group chooses their 'part' of the process or project. That student is responsible for his or her part and is graded on how well that part is completed. Teachers must sign off on each student's part and ensure the assignment is within that student's capabilities.

20	Each student completes a self-evaluation. Students will score their own efforts toward the success of the group project.
20	Each student evaluates his or her group. See the handout "Group Processing: How did we do?"
60	Teacher evaluates the group's completed assignment based on teamwork and final product.
100	Total possible points for "group grade"

This is an individual grade	Optional based on the maturity and trustworthiness of the group: Each student evaluates every other student in the group. They MUST explain in detail why they scored each student as they did.
	This grade may be combined with each student's individual grade, or be a separate grade altogether.

With this model, each student earns two or three grades for a group assignment. Each student gets one or two individual grades and a group grade. This model rewards students who work as a team and take responsibility for their part of the process and provides a logical consequence for students who do the minimum.

Behavior Management for Small Groups & Acceleration Centers

Avoiding difficult tasks is one of the most common functions of student behavior problems. With this in mind, it's important, when planning activities students must do either independently or in small groups, to assign activities within the student's range of ability. Some things to consider when setting up and implementing independent and small-group activities are:

- Provide instruction and activities that match students of varying skill levels.
- Assess student progress frequently by monitoring student work and error patterns to identify what needs to be re-taught.
- Provide a means for co-teachers and support staff to scan student work so errors can be caught early, hopefully avoiding student frustration and misbehavior.
- Avoid using worksheets as the primary focus of small-group work and Acceleration Centers. Worksheets should be kept to a minimum, if not eliminated altogether.
- Establish nonverbal signals or cues to redirect students to return to task or improve behavior.
- Establish clear routines for students to follow. Model and practice these routines.
- Notice positive behavior. Research indicates that teachers should give students more positive comments than negative comments.
- Calmly, quietly, and quickly approach and redirect students who are off task. Use an established nonverbal cue or a cue card (see cue card example).
- Use proximity control. The co-teaching environment makes this much more doable.
- Ignore misbehavior that is rewarded by teacher attention.

Have students owe time if they waste time.

Step one. Identify the behaviors that will result in the student owing time.

Step two. Discuss the situation with the offending student

Step three. Determine how much time the student will owe. Typically, an effective way to determine the time a student owes is to determine how much time they wasted or cost other students or the teacher. In this way, the student can directly correlate the consequence to restitution.

Step four. Determine when the student will serve the time that is owed (for example, after school, before school, during study hall, during recess, etc.).

Step five. Determine what form restitution will take. What can the student do to "make it up" to peers, teachers, etc.? For example, the student may be required to plan and present a lesson to the class.

Behavior Management Cue Card

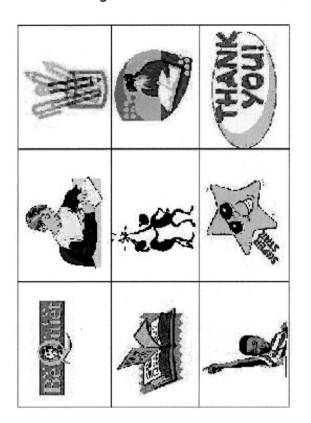

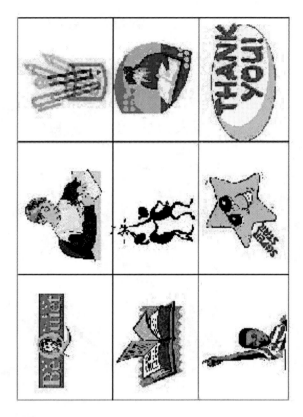

Copyright 2009 Susan Fitzell
Download color copy at www.aimhieducational.com/inclusion.aspx
click on the tab: Learned Helplessness/Behavior Management

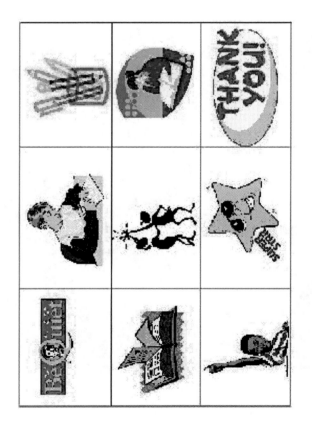

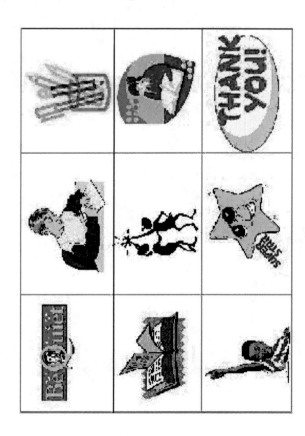

Behavior management cue card instructions:

1. Print out this card or your own version of the card.

2. Choose your method:

    a. Tape a card on the upper right corner of each student desk.
        i.   Laminate the card.
        ii. Use clear shipping tape to secure it to the desk.

    b. Hang it from a lanyard around your neck or keep it in your pocket.
        i.   Laminate the card.
        ii. Punch a hole in the top of the card to hang from a lanyard.

3. Explain the card to the students. You might say, "I want to use a system to help students stay on track without embarrassing students by saying something out loud. I also want a way to praise students and let them know that I'm pleased with good behavior and choices without causing embarrassment. So I'm going to use this card to let you know my expectations or give kudos quietly. Here is an example of the card and what the pictures mean."

    a. Explain what each picture means.
    b. Explain that you do not expect students to say anything in response.
    c. Explain how you will use the card:

4. When a student needs to be redirected, simply walk quietly up to the student.

5. Make eye contact – and preferably smile. The point is to minimize the possibility that a power struggle will ensue.

6. After eye contact is made with the student, point to the picture that sends the message you need to deliver.

7. Do not wait for a response.

8. Turn around and walk away.

9. If a student chooses to say something in response to a redirection, they are inviting a power struggle.

10. Avoid taking the bait if at all possible. Turn and walk away and wait to see if the student complies.

11. When a student earns praise, simply walk up to the student, make eye contact, smile, and point to the 'praise' picture.

12. Do not wait for a response.

13. Turn around and walk away.

Be generous with your praise. Students should receive 5-7 positive statements from the teacher in ratio to each negative comment.

Positive Reinforcement for Small Groups and Acceleration Centers

Depending on the grade you are teaching, the type of positive reinforcement you might choose will be different. Sixth-graders might respond well to earning points or tickets for positive behavior. You might also try having a bar graph for each group on the table that can be filled in as students progress toward completion of an assignment. Once the bar graph is filled in, students earn a reward.

Older students also respond well to earning points, or even stickers, for positive behavior. I have seen high school students compete aggressively with each other to see who could earn the most stickers. Points or stickers can be traded in for a free homework pass for everyone in the group, or students can put their name in a bucket for a raffle and the prize could be a free homework pass or extra time on the computer or some other privilege that your students are motivated by.

The bottom line is that the most important factor in managing behavior is responding to problem behavior consistently.

Reflection Notes

Team Teaching

Teacher 1

Teacher 2

Team teaching is not 'tag team' teaching

Both teach the class at the same time

Both teach equally with a dialogue going back and forth, or taking turns presenting information while the other assesses the group's understanding to pipe in with clarification, visuals, etc.

Team Teaching

Last but not least is team teaching, an advanced method of co-teaching. This approach usually requires that both teachers feel competent in the subject area.

Co-teachers can equally present the content being taught, ask critical thinking questions, play 'devil's advocate' in order to make a point, debate with each other and the students, and take advantage of both teachers' knowledge of the subject. Students clearly see no difference in hierarchy between the co-teachers using this approach. Teachers often find this approach satisfying, stimulating, and fun. Students are usually stimulated and motivated by having this double dynamic in the classroom. Some co-teachers become so effective in planning and working together that they feel their work is cut in half using a team teaching approach.

Normally, team teaching does not occur unless both teachers are comfortable with each other. Usually they have been together for a while and know the topic equally well.

There are exceptions, such as when there are two people that click. This can happen in English or social studies. They're comfortable with each other. They both read the story, banter off each other, talk about each other, talk about different points, and they share the classroom equally. Sometimes they don't even have time to plan together, but they can still pull it off. It just depends on the personalities, but usually this situation occurs when teachers are very comfortable with each other and both know the content equally well.

It can be fun when you have reached the level where you can truly team teach. You play off one another, team with one another, and support each other. It can be amazing to watch an expert team managing the behavior and the instruction and the activities all at once. When the two teachers really jell, and they both know the subject well, team teaching is something to behold.

Benefits of Team Teaching

- Creates effective, fun learning
- Teachers can use their knowledge effectively together
- Keeps co-teacher involved in class
- Allows for shared ideas including enrichment and differentiation
- Breaks up the monotony of one person doing all instruction
- Creates many spontaneous teachable moments

Studies have shown that when students in general education have co-teachers, they don't always make significant gains with team teaching. However, they do enjoy the class more. They're more motivated; they love it. They may meet the other teacher in the halls and say, "How come you're not in my other class?" The dynamics going on in the classroom keep students interested and motivated.

Challenges of Team Teaching

- Co-teachers must click, not conflict
- Requires supporting and carrying 100 percent of the load by both teachers
- Both teachers may have to be equally involved in the planning, grading, correcting, and supporting in the classroom
- Unless they are at the stage where they are finishing each other's sentences, planning may take a long time

How do co-teachers decide which approach to use?

Co-teaching works best when educators make conscious choices about how to implement the co-teaching model. Each approach has benefits and challenges that should be considered for each lesson or class period. It's also important to consider the co-teachers' personalities and learning styles. Co-teaching doesn't work well when two teachers show up in a room together and 'punt.'

One teacher, one support teacher is the most common co-teaching model; however, any one of the other models might be a better choice depending on the lesson plan, the class dynamics, available preparation time, availability of materials, and so on and so forth. Some models are more appropriate for certain grade levels or subject areas, or at certain times of the year, than others.

Choose models based on the goals of the lesson, class personality, behavioral dynamics, and teacher comfort levels. Consider the benefits and challenges to each model and then decide, with your co-teacher, what will work best. It is not uncommon to observe seasoned co-teachers using one model the first half of the class, another co-teaching model the second half, and a totally different co-teaching model the following day.

Co-teachers might choose approaches based on:

The learning needs of the students, student behavior, and the level of student motivation.

Teacher personality and learning style can significantly impact which approach is chosen. A teacher may prefer alternative teaching to team teaching, for example. The lesson plan often dictates which approach might work best. If the lesson involves hands-on small-group work, teachers may choose station teaching or alternative teaching. If the lesson is primarily direct teaching, teachers might choose team teaching or have one teach while one supports.

The physical space available in the classroom may significantly impact station teaching, parallel teaching, or alternative teaching. Sometimes teachers have to be very creative in order to figure out a way to differentiate presentation styles within the physical limitations of the classroom.

The Bottom Line on Co-Teaching Models & Differentiated Instruction

If we want to achieve inclusion in our classrooms, let's examine the choice of implementation method. We cannot expect to be teaching the whole class all the time. If you attempt to do so, you will not see the gains you are looking for <u>no matter how many</u> adults you have in the room. This is especially true if the class is teacher-directed with the students copying notes provided by the teacher.

This is because of who your "inclusion" students are:

- Those on an IEP
- Students whose first language is not English (the language of instruction)
- Those on a 504 plan
- Students who are not responding

They are struggling because they are unable to learn in the traditional, auditory-based, lecture-based, whole-class, everybody-does-the-same-thing-at-the-same-time teaching approach. Sure, students who *can* learn auditorily and through verbal linguistic strategies will do fine. We are not doing this for them; they are already learning. We are trying to reach the subgroups that are not making necessary gains.

Discussion Points

Discuss with your co-teacher how you might use parallel teaching and alternative teaching to effectively meet the wide range of ability levels in your classroom.

- When might parallel or alternative teaching be appropriate?
- What topics might lend themselves to parallel or alternative teaching?
- How might this approach allow focus on high achievers, on-level students, and low achievers?

Discuss with your co-teacher how you might use station teaching and team teaching to effectively meet the wide range of ability levels in your classroom.

- Which approach do you feel would be the hardest to do? Why?
- What benefit can you see for co-teaching in each of these approaches?
- Which of all the approaches would you be more willing to try first? Why?

Co-Teaching and Inclusion and Student Numbers

A common question asked when a district puts inclusion and co-teaching into place is, "How many students with special needs should be placed in the general education classroom?" There is no black and white answer to this question; however, it's important to first clarify terms and then address the issue.

Usually, the question of how many students with special needs to include in the general education classroom is more a function of the inclusion process than the co-teaching process. Remember that co-teaching is not inclusion and inclusion is not co-teaching. First let's define inclusion.

Inclusion is a concept whereby students with disabilities should be participants in the educational life of the regular classroom. The concept claims inclusion is an inherent right of the student and values this participation as a foundation of the educational experience for all students.

1993 IDEA findings and current research forced a push towards inclusion.

Types of Inclusion:

Full Inclusion	Responsible Inclusion
• Placement takes precedence over individual needs	• Placement is individualized and needs-based
• Placement in regular classrooms is an end in itself	• Placement is a means to an end: appropriate educational program
• Recommends <u>one type of placement for all children</u> and downplays the use of any alternative settings for instructional purposes	• Emotionally and behaviorally disordered students are only placed in a regular classroom when appropriate support is in place.

While there is no explicit percentage or ratio that defines the ideal inclusion classroom, typically one would want less than 50% of the students on an IEP as part of the general education classroom roster. More ideally, the percentage might be 25% of students at risk or on an IEP and 75% average to gifted. The difficulty is that school districts rarely have enough staffing and/or funding to adequately support the ideal inclusion environment. Because of these issues and scheduling concerns, schools often struggle with the following:

Placing all students on an IEP and all at-risk students in the same classroom

This does not result in inclusion. Rather, it is another form of a self-contained class and segregating the lowest level students out of the general population. While this may seem to make sense because students are all of similar academic level and the classroom could be well staffed, it creates a class where there are fewer positive role models for behavior, where there are fewer students thinking on the higher levels of Bloom's taxonomy participating in discussions, where self-esteem and morale are lower because students know they're in the 'dummy class,' and finally, where test scores remain low because of typically lower standards in the classroom. According to research, when we put low-level students together in the same classroom they achieve a percentile gain of -23% (Marzano, 2001).

Spreading students with special needs evenly between all classroom teachers

Some districts attempt to distribute students amongst the classes in a "one-for-you, one-for-you" approach. The difficulty that arises from this approach is that schools rarely have enough staffing to have every class co-taught. Consequently, general classroom teachers are under-supported in this model. Special education teachers are spread too thin and services to students with special needs end up lacking.

When a district I was teaching in first instituted inclusion in the high school, two to three classrooms in every core subject area were chosen to be co-taught. Students with special needs were then placed into each of these co-taught classrooms. English, math, social studies, and science had specific classrooms designated as inclusion co-taught classrooms. Because we had a high percentage of students with special needs in the district, each of these classrooms had between 10 and 13 students on an IEP. Class sizes ranged from 27 to 33 students. What this meant was that some classrooms had almost 50% of the population with special needs. Classroom teachers felt that the numbers of students on an IEP in the classroom were too high.

After two years of lobbying that students with special needs should be spread out amongst more classrooms, the administration chose to add more inclusion classrooms for each subject area. However, the district budget did not allow for additional special-education staff. Consequently, there was not enough staff to co-teach in all the classrooms that were designated as inclusion classrooms. Classroom teachers, however, still required support for students with special needs. In order to deal with minimal staffing, the special-education staff ended up being scheduled so that they might be in one classroom three days a week and another classroom two days a week. Co-teachers quickly realized that this situation made it much more difficult to effectively co-teach because planning time was reduced, consistency was lacking, specialists did not know what was happening in the classroom from one day to the next, and student follow-up suffered. Some teachers decided they would prefer to have a larger percentage of students on an IEP in the classroom and have a co-teacher always there. Unfortunately, that sentiment came too late.

Eventually, the demands placed on special education staff made their placement in the co-teaching environment even more difficult so, rather than co-teach, the school moved to a consult model. Each department was assigned one special educator to cover all the classes. Paraprofessionals were placed in some classrooms for support, and all teachers had fully-included classrooms. This model was the least desirable because classroom teachers did not feel adequately supported. Students were less able to have their needs met because there wasn't a certified teacher in the room to assist in planning, differentiating instruction, and adapting and modifying curriculum.

The moral of the story is, be careful what you wish for.

Effective methods of distributing students in co-taught classrooms:

- Handpicking the students and the teachers for specific classrooms.

- Consciously choose student combinations. For example, avoid putting students with significant disabilities in the same classrooms as students with serious behavioral problems.

- Avoid putting students who 'feed off' each other together (these are often students who have been in the same self-contained classroom over the years).

- Avoid class combinations where most of the students are on an IEP, a 504 plan, or at-risk with only a few students who are higher achieving. This combination not only shortchanges the students with academic needs but also shortchanges the students who are at higher levels of achievement.

- When placing students in a classroom, consider the other services they might need and how service providers might need to coordinate in order to provide those services. Generally, it may not be wise to put all the students who need speech therapy in the same classroom; however, you must consider specialist schedules and how class placement affects the ability of the specialists to provide services.

- When schedules are computerized it will probably be necessary to hand-schedule students with special needs either before or after the master schedule is completed.

Scheduling Co-Teaching

Reflection Notes

Scheduling co-teaching can be extremely difficult, especially at the secondary level. At the elementary level the challenge is usually a lack of special education staff to co-teach daily at each academic grade level where inclusion is the desired approach. At the middle school level, school schedules provide challenges because of requirements for highly qualified teachers at each grade level to be content area certified as well as the multitude of classrooms that may need co-teaching support. The challenge is greatest in states where highly qualified status requires a special education teacher to be content area certified also. Not all states require this. In some states, as long as the general education teacher is highly qualified, the special education teacher does not need to be. If the special education teacher does not need to be highly qualified in the content area in order to co-teach, that teacher might be able to support several subject areas. If a special education teacher must be highly qualified in the content area in order to co-teach, that teacher is usually only available to teach in one or possibly two content areas.

Some possible models for scheduling co-teaching are shown in the following diagrams.

Co-teaching every day – Middle School Level

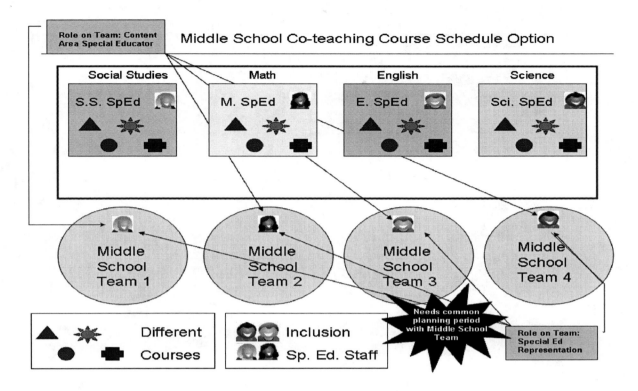

Co-teaching every day by department – High School Level

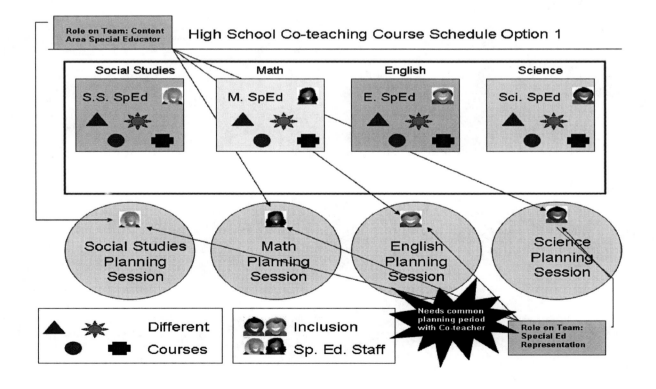

Co-teaching every other day, multi-class – High School Level

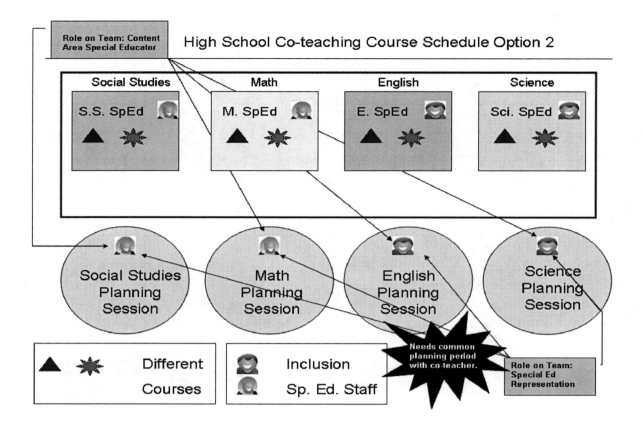

High School Co-teaching Course Schedule Option 2

Co-teaching Scheduling Option 1

Teacher	Period A	Period B	Period C	Period D	Period E	Period F	Period G
	Co-taught Social Studies	Co-taught Social Studies	Resource	Lunch	Prep & Co-plan	Co-taught Social Studies	Co-taught Social Studies
	Co-taught Math	Resource	Co-taught Math	Co-taught Math	Lunch	Prep & Co-plan	Co-taught Math
	Resource	Co-taught English	Co-taught English	Prep & Co-plan	Co-taught English	Lunch	Co-taught English
	Co-taught Science	Co-taught Science	Prep & Co-plan	Resource	Lunch	Co-taught Science	Co-taught Science

Co-teaching Scheduling Option 2

Teacher	Period A	Period B	Period C	Period D	Period E	Period F	Period G
	Co-taught Social Studies	Co-taught Math	Resource	Lunch	Prep & Co-plan	Co-taught Social Studies	Co-taught Math
	Co-taught English	Resource	Co-taught English	Co-taught Science	Lunch	Prep & Co-plan	Co-taught Science

Scheduling options 1 & 2 are the most effective co-teaching options if and when administration can prevent the co-taught classes from becoming disproportionately filled with students with special needs. Being in the classroom five days per week provides the most consistency. The maximum percentage of students with special needs in a co-taught or inclusion class is approximately 40%. Even 40% can be too high a percentage if that 40% is significantly disabled. Preferably, that 40% is a mix of students with mild to moderate learning disabilities. When too many students have significant needs or are highly involved, the inclusion model becomes strained and potentially ineffective.

 (40% is based on my professional experience with co-teaching and inclusion. Presently, there is no specific data on the 'ideal' percentage. If schools had plentiful budgets and enough special education staff was available, I would aim for a maximum of 25% of students with special needs in the inclusion or co-taught classroom.)

Co-teaching Scheduling Option 3

Teacher	Period A	Period B	Period C	Period D	Period E	Period F	Period G
	(M, W) Co-taught Social Studies (T, TH) Co-taught Math	(M, W) Co-taught Social Studies (T, TH) Co-taught Math	Resource	Lunch	Prep & Co-plan	(M, W) Co-taught Social Studies (T, TH) Co-taught Math	(M, W) Co-taught Social Studies (T, TH) Co-taught Math
	Friday: Float	Friday: Float	Resource	Friday: Float	Friday: Float	Friday: Float	Friday: Float
	(W, F) Co-taught English (T, TH) Co-taught Science	Resource	W, F) Co-taught English (T, TH) Co-taught Science	W, F) Co-taught English (T, TH) Co-taught Science	Lunch	Prep & Co-plan	W, F) Co-taught English (T, TH) Co-taught Science
	Monday: Float	Resource	Monday: Float	Monday: Float	Monday: Float	Monday: Float	Monday: Float

On a "float" day, teachers co-teach, consult, attend meetings, plan with co-teachers, etc. as necessary. Teacher chooses when to have lunch & prep.

Special Education teachers have different "float" days in order to provide maximum coverage for I.E.P. meetings, & consulting in non-resource classrooms.

Caution: A float day should not be used as a once-a-week full day prep.

Co-teaching Scheduling Option 4

Teacher	Period A	Period B	Period C	Period D	Period E	Period F	Period G
	(M, W) Co-taught Social Studies (T, TH) Co-taught Math	(M, W) Co-taught Social Studies (T, TH) Co-taught Math	Resource	Lunch	Prep & Co-plan	(M, W) Co-taught Social Studies (T, TH) Co-taught Math	(M, W) Co-taught Social Studies (T, TH) Co-taught Math
	Friday: In class consult	Friday: In class consult	Resource	Lunch	Prep & Co-plan	Friday: In class consult	Friday: In class consult
	(W, F) Co-taught English (T, TH) Co-taught Science	Resource	W, F) Co-taught English (T, TH) Co-taught Science	W, F) Co-taught English (T, TH) Co-taught Science	Lunch	Prep & Co-plan	W, F) Co-taught English (T, TH) Co-taught Science
	Monday: In class consult	Resource	Monday: In class consult	Monday: In class consult	Lunch	Prep & Co-plan	Monday: In class consult

In class consult: Teachers are assigned to a specific class that needs support yet does not require full time co-teaching. For example, a special education teacher consults with a general education teacher who has a small number of students with special needs in the class whereas those students do not need daily support.

Co-teaching is possible during 'in class consult' periods if the general education teacher sets up Acceleration Centers™ and uses that time for center work. Acceleration Centers ™ are ideal for this situation. See the section on academic strategies for instructions on how to implement Acceleration Centers ™. Acceleration Centers ™ also work well for the two-day-per-week co-teach model.

Questions to Consider when Preparing to Teach Together

Planning time

How much time do we need to plan?

When will we make the time to plan?

What checks can we put in place to ensure we use our time effectively?

What documentation or materials should we bring to the planning meeting with us?

Instruction

How will we determine the content to be taught? Will we use curriculum compacting, curriculum mapping data, or state standards to target the most critical content?

Who will plan what?

When will the special education co-teacher implement instruction to students with disabilities, without disabilities, both?

How will the co-teacher implement instruction?

How will we decide who teaches what?

Who creates curriculum adaptations, accommodations, and modifications?

Who adapts the tests?

How will we use our strengths in the classroom when planning instruction?

How will we present the content? Will one person do all the direct teaching or will both share responsibility for teaching the lesson?

Should we rotate responsibilities?

If working with a paraprofessional, who will train the paraprofessional to use the specific instruction strategies?

Who will evaluate the effectiveness of the instruction provided by the paraprofessional?

Student Behavior

What are the classroom expectations (i.e., classroom rules) for students and adults?

How are classroom expectations communicated to the students?

What is the plan to address unacceptable student behavior in a timely manner?

What are the specific roles of the adults in the room in supporting positive student behavior?

How will we be consistent in managing behavior and support each other's authority?

What are our pet peeves? What student behavior pushes our buttons? What can we not tolerate in the classroom?

If our discipline style is very different, where can we find common ground?

Communication

How will we ensure regular communication with each other?

How will we address our communication needs with each other?

Who will communicate with the parents of students on an IEP? The students who are not on an IEP? Do we share the responsibility for communication equally?

How should we handle conflict or concern with each other to preserve the harmony of our relationship?

When one of us wants to share a new idea should we present it in writing first so there's time to process or just talk about it?

Who will communicate with parents about: routine daily occurrences, unusual situations, other?

What do we need to know about each other?

What do I need in order to work effectively in my classroom?

What can I absolutely not tolerate in my co-teacher?

What am I looking forward to in the co-teaching relationship?

What are my non-negotiables?

The most important thing to me in our co-teaching relationship is…?

What are our expectations of each other?

How do we react to unexpected changes in plans?

What are our expectations regarding:

- Class work and homework being done on time, or independently?
- Grading?
- Noise level?
- Small-group work?
- Differentiating instruction?
- Giving or receiving feedback?
- Dividing the work load?

Co-Teaching Preparation Questionnaire

Planning time: When will we plan and how much time will we need per session? What should we bring with us?

_____

_____

_____

Instruction:

What will we teach? _____

Who will plan what? _____

What approach will we use? _____

Who will teach what? _____

Who will create curriculum adaptations, accommodations, modifications, and test adaptations?

_____

Student behavior:

Are the ground rules clearly defined and understood by the class? _____

How will we address behavior issues and support each other's authority?

_____

_____

What pet peeves or student behaviors can you not tolerate in the classroom?

_____

_____

Communication:

How can we ensure regular communication and address our needs with each other?

_____

_____

Who will be responsible for interacting with the parent of students on an IEP?

_____

Who will be responsible for interacting with parents on routine issues?

_____

What's the best way for others to share new ideas with you? _____

_____

How should we handle issues or concerns with each other to minimize conflict?

_____

_____

Personal:

What do we need to know about each other to work effectively together?

_____

_____

_____

What are you looking forward to and what can you not tolerate in your co-teacher?

_____

_____

What are your non-negotiable issues? _____

_____

What is the most important thing to you in a co-teaching relationship?

_____

_____

Expectations:

Timeliness of class work and homework _____

_____

Students working independently or collaboratively _____

_____

Grading _____

Noise level in the classroom

_____

Small group work

_____

Differentiating

instruction_____

Giving & receiving feedback _____

Dividing the work load _____

Notes:

Roles & Responsibilities for Co-Teaching (Sample Example)

Classroom Teacher

- Develop the structure of the class, including general curricula, discipline policy, physical layout, materials, etc. in collaboration with the co-teacher.
- Plan daily lessons, activities, tests, assignments, etc. in collaboration with the special education teacher.
- Supervise and direct paraprofessionals in the classroom routine.
- Collaborate with the special educator on curriculum modifications, grading, report cards, grade transitions, etc.
- Collaborate with full team including parents and students.
- Implement adaptations, modifications, and accommodations required by the IEP.

Special Education Teacher

- Provide modification recommendations for students in regard to materials and equipment, positive behavior plans, individualized curricula, etc.
- Provide modification recommendations for students in regard to lessons, activities, tests, assignments, grading, report cards, etc.
- Recommend instructional strategies for students.
- Collaborate with the classroom teacher to develop discipline policy.
- Collaborate with the classroom teacher to develop lesson plans for the whole class, where appropriate.
- Work directly with students on an individual or group basis.
- Work individually with students as they are doing class work, and help as necessary.
- Teach specific skills. Re-teach as necessary for individual students.
- Adapt or modify regular classroom materials, tests, and assignments.
- IEP development with classroom teacher input.

Paraprofessional

- Follow classroom policies developed by the classroom teacher.
- Implement modifications developed by the team.
- Provide direct instruction and facilitate learning opportunities for individuals and groups of students as planned by teacher or specialist.
- Provide assistance to all students.
- Re-teach specific skills as necessary.
- Coordinate IEP modifications (sharing information and recommendations

between specialist and classroom teacher).
- Follow classroom policies developed by the classroom teacher.
- Implement modifications developed by the team.
- Provide direct instruction and facilitate learning opportunities for individuals and groups of students as planned by teacher or specialist.
- Provide assistance to all students.
- Chart progress (academically and behaviorally) for all students.

When co-teaching is not possible, special education teachers act as liaisons for the content area teacher. In that capacity, the general classroom teacher implements adaptations to meet IEP requirements per IDEA. The special education teacher provides consultation to the content area teacher to help implement IEP requirements.

How Do We Introduce Ourselves?

Co-teaching requires educators to think differently about their roles in the classroom. One of the best ways to introduce co-teaching pairs to students in the classroom is content area specialist (math, science, English, social studies, etc.) and learning strategies specialist (special education teacher). Other co-teaching pairs choose not to introduce their expertise at all but rather announce themselves as being the teachers in the classroom.

The least recommended option is to announce that one teacher is the math teacher, for example, and the other teacher is a special education teacher. It is not even recommended that students are told the special education teacher is there for the students with special needs. When a co-teaching pair specifies who is "the real teacher" and who is "the special education teacher" an immediate hierarchy is established and stigma begins to form for students with special needs in the classroom. This stigma can be bad enough to cause students who need assistance to refuse it for fear of being labeled "sped."

Planning Time

Planning time is sacred. Repeat: planning time is sacred. If it's built into your schedule, it is not a time for you to be pulled out to go to an IEP meeting.

I know that's not the real world, but at least it should not be the norm. This means that we, as special education teachers, and we, as general education

Reflection Notes

teachers, need to push back on the people scheduling those meetings and say, "Do it another time." Because if you don't have time to plan together, when are you going to be able to make this co-teaching relationship work?

Now, I have to qualify this. I've been in school districts where the teachers actually had a time every single day to plan together, and they did have to be pulled from that period occasionally for a meeting. However, they did have four other days. I could plan with my co-teacher in one or two planning periods a week, and sometimes, if we really used our time well, we could do two weeks of lesson plans in 45 minutes.

How did we do that? We planned ahead. We came to the meeting with lesson plans sketched out, and we used that time to determine accommodations and adaptations. We input activities and suggestions into the general plan for the curriculum. Then we arranged to meet again two or three days later for 45 minutes to revisit the plan.

We did some of the work outside of the planning period and came ready with an outline for changes. That made planning much more efficient.

Once the administrator came to me after a coaching session in his school district and said, "They have planning time every single day, so if we have to schedule an IEP meeting during that meeting, they should be able to handle it." That was an administrator's point of view, and I have to agree. So, although it's sacred, we have to use our professional judgment.

How do you co-teach when you don't have conference or planning time together? Some of the co-teaching models require minimal planning time. Some require extensive planning time. Choose the model that you can support. Ask yourself, "How do I fit common planning time in my schedule?"

When I was at the high school level we were able to plan one unit at a time. We planned a whole unit ahead and a unit could take a week or sometimes two. We didn't have common planning time. Whenever we had to plan, I would go in at 6:00 a.m. to plan with one of my co-teaching teams. Luckily, there were three of us teaching the same topic, and because we had to share materials, we all planned together. We did not have enough lab materials for everyone to teach the same topic at the same time, so we would alternate days with the materials. I was actually able to plan with my co-teachers for two or three periods at a time. In some situations we might meet during my lunch, and either give up lunch, and/or plan with a working lunch. In other situations I gave up a prep if I could.

Sometimes we can get upset about the fact that it's not built into our school day, or even if it is built into our school day, we may not use it to the best of our ability. Are we planning or are we using the time to talk about how bad Johnny was in class last period? When we make time to plan we need to discuss who will teach what, who adapts the test, how do we handle discipline, what things are the non-negotiables?

If you are working with a team or a co-teacher, you need time to plan together. If you don't have the time to discuss plans, review upcoming tests, and consider recommended modifications and the implementation of IEP goals, it will be difficult, if not impossible, to have a successful co-taught classroom.

If your school provides you with planning time, stay focused on the task at hand. Try to avoid social conversation because it will leave you feeling like you accomplished nothing afterwards.

If possible, share information beforehand through your school's teacher mailboxes or email so your planning time can be used with maximum benefit.

Speak up if you are being asked to give up planning time for other duties. You need that time and it is legitimate to require it. If your school does not provide planning time, it will probably make your life easier in the long run if you can employ some of the following options:

- Use time before school, after school, or during common preps/specials to meet and plan. Remember, the goal is to make YOUR job easier and more successful in the long run. It is a waste of your energy to begrudge the time spent if you choose this option.

- Arrange for coverage with a substitute one day a week or month to free up collaboration time. Some schools hire permanent substitutes to cover for co-teachers so they can plan during the day rather than before or after school.

- Contact your local PTA and see if there are parent volunteers who may be willing to help cover classes so you can plan. High schools seriously under-utilize volunteers. To bridge the gap between academics and the world of work it could even be beneficial to have parents or community members cover a class by presenting real-life applications from their own job experience for the students in the classroom.**

- Partner with colleges and universities to have students who are studying to be teachers present activities, provide demonstrations, review with games, and help with test prep to free up time for co-teachers to plan.**

- **Teachers will need to plan in the room because of liability issues; however, it's a viable option when planning time is scarce.

- Some schools pay co-teachers a stipend to plan after school. Other options are to compensate co-teachers for planning during the school vacation week or during summer hours.

- Much of what is talked about in a faculty meeting can be presented in a memo. When possible, use faculty meeting time to allow co-teachers to work on long-range plans, problem solving, and future lesson outlines and establish a framework for collaborating over the next month.

- When the special educator in the co-teaching pair co-teaches with more than one general education teacher, choose one day a week, for example, Fridays, to leave each class period 15 minutes early. Then use that time to plan with one of the general education teachers who is free at that time. For example, first period of the day, James, a special education teacher, leaves Allen's math class 15 minutes early and meets with Michael, the general education teacher he works with fourth period because it's Michael's prep period at that time.

- Some schools set up targeted activity periods for students to review for proficiency testing, cooperative learning groups, or peer tutoring to allow time for teachers to plan together. These targeted activity periods can be monitored by support staff or school specialists.

- Substitutes often have free blocks of time when the teacher they are substituting for has prep periods. Schedule a substitute to cover your class during that free block of time.

- For information that must be communicated before the next school day, you might arrange to call each other after hours. At the least, communicate through the school mailbox or email.

- If the regular classroom teacher can provide the special education teacher with copies of lesson plans, tests, and projects ahead of time, it allows time for the specialist to assist with accommodations and make helpful recommendations. It also enables that person to go into the class prepared to help.

- Placing grade reports in the special education teacher's mailbox enables both the regular classroom teacher and the special education teacher to catch failures before they become quarterly or semester grades.

- Use email and Microsoft Word's "Insert Comments & Track Changes" features to collaborate on accommodations and adaptations.

IEP-Based Planning Form

CONFIDENTIAL

Student   Grade

Learning Style   Multiple
                                        Intelligence

Interests

Strengths   Challenges

Notes/Reminders:

Class Activity	Student Activity	Goals/Mods Met	Supports Needed

Other:

Differentiated Planning: Lesson Planner

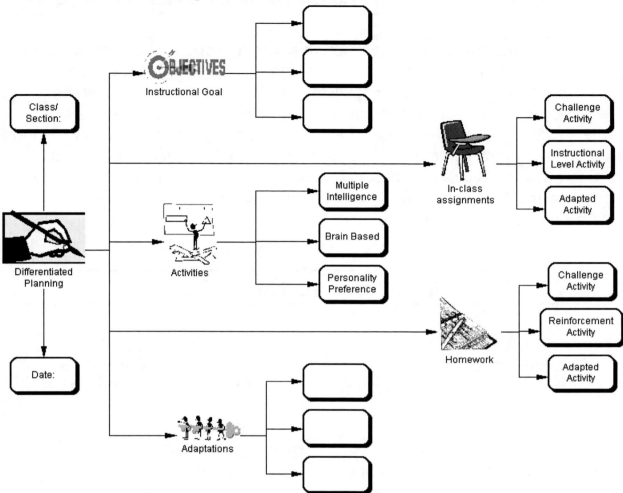

Goal:

Date	Activities	Adaptations	In-Class Assign	Homework

Assessment:

Communication and an Organized Approach

One of the most important aspects of an effective working relationship between the paraprofessional, special educator, teacher, or specialist is clear and consistent communication and organization. It is critical to communicate frequently and use organizing tools that can help define roles, define expectations, and set parameters for class norms as part of the communication process. Why is structure and time to talk so important? Because without having a system in place to discuss issues, organize information, and handle variables, much is subject to guesswork, and guesswork often causes problems and communication breakdown.

How Is Co-Teaching Going?

The following is a list of questions to ask yourselves when trying to evaluate your co-teaching process. Ideally, co-teachers meet to discuss and evaluate progress twice a month. Make a date to have this conversation and stick to it!

- Are students on an IEP reaching higher standards?
- Are general education students reaching higher standards?
- Are you teaching to the middle or to the lower achievers?
- Are you using station teaching and flexible grouping to allow all students to accelerate learning, including the students at the top of the class?
- Do students know who is designated as special education?
- Do they feel both teachers are there to help all students?
- Do they see both teachers as equals?
- Are there social and behavioral benefits?
- How will you determine students' perceptions of your co-taught class?
- Are you communicating?
- Are you feeling fulfilled in your co-teaching experience?
- Do both teachers believe their skills are valued and used to maximize student success in the classroom?
- Are you differentiating instruction?
- Do you feel the workload division is fair and consistent?
- What would you like to see improved?
- What are you doing well?
- What needs to change?
- Are you making time to plan together?

- Is planning time being used effectively?

Is administration aware of how the co-taught process is going in your classroom? How will you keep administration informed? When there are positive gains in student achievement directly related to the co-teaching process, be sure that administration is aware. Provide documentation and feedback.

More than one successful co-teaching pair has lamented that their co-taught class was reassigned or eliminated because of an administrative decision. Sometimes, that decision is made because administration is unaware of how the relationship is contributing to student success and higher state test scores.

On the flip side, administration cannot support resolution of obstacles to the co-teaching process if they are unaware of what those roadblocks are. When presenting concerns to administration, be sure to present possible solutions. When administration does not see the successes or problems in a co-teaching situation, they are unable to support the process.

Co-teaching Observation Form

The following form is a tool for observing the co-teaching process. Provide the tool to a trusted peer or administrator and ask for objective feedback on how the co-teaching process is progressing in your classroom. It's difficult to assess how well we are doing when on the 'inside.' Objective feedback can be invaluable to improving your process.

CO-TEACHING OBSERVATION FORM

CO-TEACHER NAMES: Content_____ SpEd_____ Subject:_____ Other:_____ Date:_____

Start time:_____ End time:_____ Debrief time:_____

TIME	INSTRUCTIONAL MATERIALS	INSTRUCTIONAL METHODS/CO-TEACH APPROACH	STUDENT SKILL REQUEST	CO-TEACHER ROLE: (Instructing/Assisting)	STUDENT BEHAVIOR & # ENGAGED	COMMENTS/QUESTIONS

Use space to diagram classroom to provide feedback on structure/engagement.

Instructional Methods: Small Group (SG), Whole Group (WG), Individualized (I), Varied (V)
Co-teaching approaches: 1 teach/1 support (1), Station (ST), Parallel (P), Alternative (A), Team (T)

Suggestions are on reverse side.
Suggestions are options – NOT should haves!

One-Page Planning Form

Approx. 45 min class period	Time	One-Page Planning Form
M		
Content Standard(s) Addressed:		
Co-teaching approach (Circle)		1 teach/1 support , Station , Parallel , Alternative , Team
Bell Ringer	5 min	
Whole Class Mini Lesson	10 min	
Target Lesson: (circle)	20 min	
Small Group, Acceleration Centers, Individualized Instruction, Varied		
Evaluation	5 min	
T		
Content Standard(s) Addressed:		
Co-teaching approach (Circle)		1 teach/1 support , Station , Parallel , Alternative , Team
Bell Ringer		
Whole Class Mini Lesson		
Target Lesson: (circle)		
Small Group, Acceleration Centers, Individualized Instruction, Varied		
Evaluation		
W		
Content Standard(s) Addressed:		
Co-teaching approach (Circle)		1 teach/1 support , Station , Parallel , Alternative , Team
Bell Ringer		
Whole Class Mini Lesson		
Target Lesson: (circle)		
Small Group, Acceleration Centers, Individualized Instruction, Varied		
Evaluation		
TH		
Content Standard(s) Addressed:		
Co-teaching approach (Circle)		1 teach/1 support , Station , Parallel , Alternative , Team
Bell Ringer		
Whole Class Mini Lesson		
Target Lesson: (circle)		
Small Group, Acceleration Centers, Individualized Instruction, Varied		
Evaluation		
F		
Content Standard(s) Addressed:		
Co-teaching approach (Circle)		1 teach/1 support , Station , Parallel , Alternative , Team
Bell Ringer		
Whole Class Mini Lesson		
Target Lesson: (circle)		
Small Group, Acceleration Centers, Individualized Instruction, Varied		
Evaluation		

Two-Page Planning Form

Approx. 45 min class period

		Time		Additional Notes, Comments, Accommodations, etc.
M	**Content Standard(s) Addressed:**			
	Co-teaching approach (Circle) 1 teach/1 support , Station , Parallel , Alternative , Team			
	Bell Ringer	5 min		
	Whole Class Mini Lesson	10 min		
	Target Lesson: (circle)	20 min		
	Small Group, Acceleration Centers, Individualized Instruction, Varied			
	Evaluation (Quiz, Exit Cards, Observation, etc.)	5 min		
T	**Content Standard(s) Addressed:**			Additional Notes, Comments, Accommodations, etc.
	Co-teaching approach (Circle) 1 teach/1 support , Station , Parallel , Alternative , Team			
	Bell Ringer			
	Whole Class Mini Lesson			
	Target Lesson: (circle)			
	Small Group, Acceleration Centers, Individualized Instruction, Varied			
	Evaluation (Quiz, Exit Cards, Observation, etc.)			
W	**Content Standard(s) Addressed:**			Additional Notes, Comments, Accommodations, etc.
	Co-teaching approach (Circle) 1 teach/1 support , Station , Parallel , Alternative , Team			
	Bell Ringer			
	Whole Class Mini Lesson			
	Target Lesson: (circle)			
	Small Group, Acceleration Centers, Individualized Instruction, Varied			
	Evaluation (Quiz, Exit Cards, Observation, etc.)			

Two-Page Planning Form   Page 2 of 2

Approx. 45 min class period

		Additional Notes, Comments, Accommodations, etc.
TH	**Content Standard(s) Addressed:**	
	Co-teaching approach (Circle) 1 teach/1 support , Station , Parallel , Alternative , Team	
	Bell Ringer	
	Whole Class Mini Lesson	
	Target Lesson: (circle)	
	Small Group, Acceleration Centers, Individualized Instruction, Varied	
	Evaluation (Quiz, Exit Cards, Observation, etc.)	
F	**Content Standard(s) Addressed:**	Additional Notes, Comments, Accommodations, etc.
	Co-teaching approach (Circle) 1 teach/1 support , Station , Parallel , Alternative , Team	
	Bell Ringer	
	Whole Class Mini Lesson	
	Target Lesson: (circle)	
	Small Group, Acceleration Centers, Individualized Instruction, Varied	
	Evaluation (Quiz, Exit Cards, Observation, etc.)	

Strategies to Differentiate Instruction implemented this week:

Things to consider when planning lessons:

- Room arrangement, additional options for space.
- What materials must be prepped ahead of time and who will prep them?
- What specific supports, aids or services do specific students need? See adaptations charts for suggestions.

Two-Page Planning Form — *Page 1 of 2*

Approx. 90 min class period

Day	Item	Time	Co-teaching approach (Circle)
M	**Content Standard(s) Addressed:**		
	Co-teaching approach (Circle)		1 teach/1 support , Station , Parallel , Alternative , Team
	Bell Ringer	5 min	
	Whole Class Mini Lesson	10 min	
	Target Lesson: (circle) Small Group, Acceleration Centers, Individualized Instruction, Varied	20 min	
	Evaluation	5 min	
	Co-teaching approach (Circle)		1 teach/1 support , Station , Parallel , Alternative , Team
	Bell Ringer	5 min	
	Whole Class Mini Lesson	10 min	
	Target Lesson: (circle) Small Group, Acceleration Centers, Individualized Instruction, Varied	20 min	
	Evaluation	5 min	
T	**Content Standard(s) Addressed:**		
	Co-teaching approach (Circle)		1 teach/1 support , Station , Parallel , Alternative , Team
	Bell Ringer	5 min	
	Whole Class Mini Lesson	10 min	
	Target Lesson: (circle) Small Group, Acceleration Centers, Individualized Instruction, Varied	20 min	
	Evaluation	5 min	
	Co-teaching approach (Circle)		1 teach/1 support , Station , Parallel , Alternative , Team
	Bell Ringer	5 min	
	Whole Class Mini Lesson	10 min	
	Target Lesson: (circle) Small Group, Acceleration Centers, Individualized Instruction, Varied	20 min	
	Evaluation	5 min	
W	**Content Standard(s) Addressed:**		
	Co-teaching approach (Circle)		1 teach/1 support , Station , Parallel , Alternative , Team
	Bell Ringer	5 min	
	Whole Class Mini Lesson	10 min	
	Target Lesson: (circle) Small Group, Acceleration Centers, Individualized Instruction, Varied	20 min	
	Evaluation	5 min	

Two-Page Planning Form — *Page 2 of 2*

Approx. 90 min class period

TH

Content Standard(s) Addressed:	
Co-teaching approach (Circle)	1 teach/1 support , Station , Parallel , Alternative , Team
Bell Ringer	5 min
Whole Class Mini Lesson	10 min
Target Lesson: (circle) Small Group, Acceleration Centers, Individualized Instruction, Varied	20 min
Evaluation	5 min
Co-teaching approach (Circle)	1 teach/1 support , Station , Parallel , Alternative , Team
Bell Ringer	5 min
Whole Class Mini Lesson	10 min
Target Lesson: (circle) Small Group, Acceleration Centers, Individualized Instruction, Varied	20 min
Evaluation	5 min

F

Content Standard(s) Addressed:	
Co-teaching approach (Circle)	1 teach/1 support , Station , Parallel , Alternative , Team
Bell Ringer	5 min
Whole Class Mini Lesson	10 min
Target Lesson: (circle) Small Group, Acceleration Centers, Individualized Instruction, Varied	20 min
Evaluation	5 min
Co-teaching approach (Circle)	1 teach/1 support , Station , Parallel , Alternative , Team
Bell Ringer	5 min
Whole Class Mini Lesson	10 min
Target Lesson: (circle) Small Group, Acceleration Centers, Individualized Instruction, Varied	20 min
Evaluation	5 min

Keeping Up With the IEP

Class List Adaptations Chart

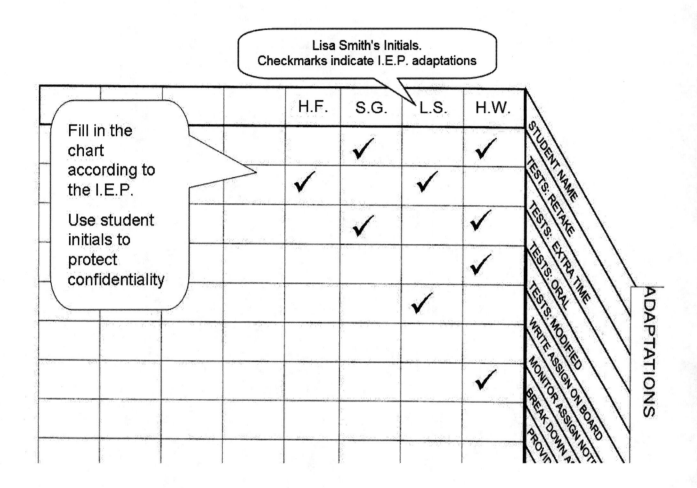

The class list adaptations chart enables teachers and paraprofessionals to remember IEP adaptations with a class snapshot.

Class List Adaptations Charts (Two variations)

Adaptations and Learning Profile – One-Page View

						⏎ Student Initials/↻Information
						Tests: Retake
						Tests: Extra Time
						Tests: Oral
						Tests: Modified
						Tests: Scribe
						Write Assignments on Board
						Monitor Assignment Notebook
						Break Down Assignments into Steps
						Provide Copies of Notes
						Substitute Hands-on for Written
						Substitute Oral for Written
						Seating Preference
						Allow Word Processor
						Allow Calculator
						Allow Text-to-Speech Software
						Allow Speech-to-Text Software
						Provide Advanced Organizer
						Needs 1 to 1 Assistance
						Visual Cues & Hands-on Critical
						Easily Overwhelmed
						Distractible
						Written Expression Weak
						Verbal Expression Weak
						Auditory Learner
						Visual Learner
						Kinesthetic Learner

Download a .PDF or .doc version of this form at
www.aimhieducational.com/inclusion.aspx

CONFIDENTIAL – Adaptations – One-Page View

	Period:		Grade:						
Subject:									
Student Initials →									
Modify Format by :									
Enlarging font									
Adding charts									
Adding pictures									
Using concrete models									
Providing books on tape									
Illustrating notes and flash cards									
Color-coding study materials									
Providing word banks									
Providing memory maps									
Flowcharting process									
Using print vs. cursive									
Using picture stories & visual directions									
Providing an outline									
Highlighting key points									
Moving from word lists to index cards									
Providing opportunity to respond orally									
Emphasizing major points (use AutoSummarize tool)									
Providing study carrel for focus									
Tape recording required reading for student									
Providing Braille									
Adapt Instruction by teaching with:									
Illustrated notes & handouts									
Color-coded teaching materials									
Memory maps									
Mnemonics									
Hands-on activities									
Assignment notebooks									
Frequent & /or immediate feedback									
Adapt Assignments by providing:									
Simplified directions									
Memory aides									
Silly rhymes to remember									
Reworded text									
Material w/reduced reading difficulty									
Reduced quantity									
Taped assignments									
Special projects in lieu of assignments									
Opportunity to leave class for assistance									
Opportunity to repeat and explain instructions									
Auditory aids (cues, tapes, etc.)									
Extra time for oral response									
Extra time for written response									
Exams of reduced length									
Oral tests									
A scribe									
Other									
Provide peer tutoring									

When schools incorporate the inclusion and co-teaching model, there are times when a special education teacher has students on his or her caseload that he or she does not see during the day. For example, I had 35 students on my caseload as well as being assigned to five co-taught classes a day. Many of those students were not in the classes to which I was assigned. Consequently, unlike the years when all students on my caseload were in my self-contained classes or resource period, I now had students that I did not ever see. I was still responsible for keeping up with their progress and monitoring their IEP. The following letters were useful for finding out how students were doing in classes where I was not assigned.

Reflection Notes

Sample Letter to Teacher to Assist With Follow-Up (Single Student)

Date: _____

Dear _____,

_____is in your _____ period
_____ class and has Academic Support Lab _____ period. Please take a moment to fill out the information below. This will assist us greatly in helping this student to be successful in your class.

Please Circle One:

1. Estimated Grade: A B C D F

2. Turns in Homework?   Always   Sometimes   Never

3. Tests/Quizzes: High   Average   Low   Failing

4. Do you feel this student could benefit from ongoing remedial instruction? If yes, please explain.

_____

_____

_____

5. Please list any assignments/tests that need to be made-up/completed.

_____

_____

Thank you for taking the time to complete this form!

Sincerely,

"Quick Form" Letter to Teachers to Assist With Follow-Up (Multiple Students)

Dear _____,

The following students are in your _____ period _____ class and have Academic Support Lab. Please take a moment to fill out the information below. This will assist us greatly in helping these students to be successful in your class. Return to _____ by _____.

Student Name	Est. Grade	Missing Homework	Missing Tests/ Quizzes	Assignments/ Tests that need make-up or completion	Comments

Part 2: Collaboration Basics
& Personality Styles

Potential Roadblocks: Challenges

What are some of the problems or obstacles that come up between the special education teacher and the classroom teacher, making it difficult to work together?

Teaching Methodology

One roadblock often evolves from a difference in how both educators approach teaching. When the personalities clash in the way a classroom is run, or if the way one teacher teaches or manages students within the classroom is very different than the other teacher's methods, it may cause conflict between the professionals.

Personality Differences

Personality differences can also be a big problem. For example, Bob was exasperated because he felt that one of the classrooms he was working with was totally out of control. The classroom teacher had a more loosely structured style of managing the classroom than was Bob's preference. Bob preferred a structured and ordered room where kids worked quietly, were orderly, did not speak out, and essentially were what we would expect from a traditional classroom: well-behaved.

The loose structure of the classroom, however, made it less likely students would be quiet or stay in their seats for any length of time. This drove Bob crazy. It created stress and conflict because he felt powerless in his position to do anything about it.

Another example of potential discord is when a classroom teacher with very strict standards about how teaching should happen in the classroom and what help a student should or should not get is paired with a special education teacher who will do anything and everything he or she can to get students to do the work. That might include cajoling, bribing, doing half of the work for them, talking to students to try to convince them to get work done, etc.

There are potential problems in either scenario, but when the two adults in the room are so very different in their approach to teaching, it is difficult to find a balance. Communication is the best solution. The special education teacher, however, may not feel comfortable having that conversation because he or she often concludes, "It is not my class, so I cannot or should not say anything about it." When co-teaching, it's both teachers' class.

Comfort Zones

Comfort zones are another significant factor in whether a relationship will be compatible. Many times, we are asked to do things in the classroom that are outside the comfort zone of either the teacher or the special education teacher in the classroom. Possibly, the IEP requires the special education teacher or the classroom teacher to use strategies that are unusual or unfamiliar. Or one of the two adults may not be comfortable sharing a classroom. When we are out of our comfort zones, we struggle.

Legal Worries

Often, the general education teacher is concerned about not meeting the educational needs of students with disabilities or the IEP requirements adequately. This is especially true when students have significant learning or physical disabilities. This can create a roadblock because the special education teacher may become the sole provider of all teaching and assistance for that student, or may even be the sole source of communication for that student.

Sometimes the classroom teacher will feel more comfortable saying, "You take care of Johnny, because you know how to deal with Johnny and I don't. I'm not a special education teacher." This is caused by a concern that the classroom teacher cannot meet the student's needs, or that legally the teacher could get into trouble if he or she takes responsibility and then cannot meet that responsibility according to the standards of the law. This belief often feeds into the attitude of, "Those SPED kids are yours."

The general education teacher is ultimately responsible for the education of the child. This is especially an issue with the current mandates of No Child Left Behind.

This Is Not the Way It Should Be

Another area of conflict and another roadblock to overcome when two adults work in a classroom together is differences in teaching styles. Often both enter the room with specific ideas of how the class should operate and how things should be. However, there is often a misperception about what is happening in the classroom, especially in the case where there has been little to no communication between these two adults prior to the first day of classes. Moreover, if class is not proceeding the way one or both of them thinks it should be, there is a problem. Again, communication is paramount in this situation. Communication simply must happen.

Credibility

Another roadblock that frequently comes up when general education teachers are working with special education teachers is one of credibility. The special education teacher is often thrown into the classroom without content area knowledge, or they may have that knowledge, but not at the same level of expertise as the general education teacher. This happens less often now because of the requirements for "highly qualified" teachers in the classroom, but it still occurs. Unfortunately, the classroom teacher may not even be aware of the special education teacher's strengths or areas of expertise, background, or his or her ability to meet the requirements of working in the general classroom.

The classroom teacher and the general education teacher both need to take the time to share their expectations with each other, to explain the teaching methods they prefer, and to rally their strengths, whether content expertise, learning strategy expertise, etc. They need to discuss how they will "be" together in the classroom and what expectations they have of each other.

Insufficient Time

If I have heard it once, I have heard it a hundred times: there is simply not enough time to prepare materials for students, to meet with the collaborating teacher to learn strategies, or to get anything done proactively for the classroom. So often, special education teachers are sent from room to room with barely enough time to eat lunch or take care of their personal needs. In addition to being overscheduled into general education classrooms, they are often expected to attend team meetings, be available immediately for crisis intervention, and do all the paperwork required of case coordinators. Often, their responsibility to a classroom teacher is disregarded by school administration or other teachers who meet them in the hall and want immediate answers to student issues.

If we want special education teachers to be effective with students with special needs in the classroom, we need to change our paradigms about planning and prep time. Districts need to take into consideration the time co-teachers and collaborating teachers need to have in order to plan together.

Lack of Administrative Support

Lack of administrative support can also be a roadblock to the success of the special education teacher working in the general education classroom. Sometimes this is simply because administrators have been unable or unwilling to provide special education teachers and general classroom teachers with collaboration and co-teaching training, time to communicate with each other, or even time to prep teaching materials. Funding can be an obstacle if there are limited monies available to provide quality training and follow-up. At times, there is a lack of support for inclusion efforts and for implementing the differentiated instruction necessary to meet the goals of No Child Left Behind. Other times, an administrator may simply have no voice amongst teachers to say loud and clear, "This is a legal requirement. We need to do it and you are accountable."

Potential Roadblocks: Other Practicalities

- At times, there is insufficient time and flexibility.
- It can be difficult to see lesson plans ahead of class time.
- There is often a lack of training in a problem-solving approach to collaboration.
- Cost of training and staffing minimizes available opportunities for professional development.
- What might you add?

Overcoming Roadblocks: Solutions

Be Flexible

Foremost, flexibility is a necessary trait for co-teachers. This can be a difficult requirement because our personalities are not always innately flexible. Some of us find it easier to go with the flow and take things as they come, or to let things roll off our backs, than others do. In the working relationship between a special education teacher and general education teacher, without flexibility, there is rigidity. With rigidity, there is often a strained relationship. Be flexible and life will be easier and your students will be better served.

Identify and Focus on Your Special Education Teacher's Strengths

The general education teacher has strengths in the classroom. The special education teacher also has strengths. Find those strengths and celebrate them. This may be one of the most viable solutions to lack of inclusion and co-teaching training. If we find our strong points, we can work with those assets without requiring additional training. It is a logical solution to a common difficulty.

Adopt a "They are all our students" Attitude

This is not only critical for the special education teacher, but also extremely important for the students with special needs within the classroom. It is especially important to work with students in the general classroom in such a way that students with special needs are not stigmatized. Stigmatization as a "SPED kid" leaves scars that can last a lifetime.

When the special education teacher takes on the ownership of a student and the general classroom teacher leaves all interactions for that student to the special education teacher, everyone loses. The general education teacher does not develop a potentially rewarding relationship with the student. The student becomes overly dependent upon the special education teacher, having less social interaction with other students and less interaction with the other adult. The student with special needs knows he or she is being ignored or left out by the general education teacher, which reinforces feelings of inferiority.

Overcoming Roadblocks: Summary & More

- Be flexible.
- Identify and focus on teacher/special education teacher strengths.
- Adopt a "They are all OUR students" attitude.
- Be self-aware.
- Assess your viewpoints of the teaching profession.
- Reflect on past experiences with change.
- Understand your stage of life and career goals.
- Consider gender and culture's impact on the relationship between you and the other adult in the classroom.
- Increase your understanding of personality types.

Perceptions & Personality

Looking at Personality Types

One of the most difficult aspects of working in the classroom with another adult is navigating personalities. Any time we work in a classroom, whether because of the personalities of our students or the adults, we will face challenges due to our differences. It is important to understand our students and how their personalities influence their learning styles. When we understand learning style, we can be more helpful to our students by teaching them to identify how they learn and enabling them to learn at their maximum capability using strategies that fit their learning style.

Most of us realize the importance of understanding student learning and personality styles. However, the importance of understanding adult personality styles is often glossed over or completely ignored in school environments. In the business world, understanding one's co-workers is often the focus of professional training.

In industry, managers, human resource departments, trainers, and team builders commonly understand the importance of understanding personality types. Sometimes businesses will even group people based on the best fit between different personalities. Schools have a tendency to simply throw people together and expect them to figure out how to collaborate and work together with virtually no training or insight into personality theory, group process, or negotiation.

When I started working with other teachers in the classroom, I quickly discovered that one of the most critical lessons I needed to learn was to understand personality styles. The first step was to understand my own personality and how my personality affected others.

When I spoke with my 'demonstrative body language', with every bit of 'passion' I possessed, with my 'extraversion' emphasizing every aspect of who I was, I intimidated people or overwhelmed some without even knowing it. It became clear to me that without an understanding of personality, I would continue to have relationships in the classroom that were not as productive as they could be. Too much time was spent misinterpreting each other, misunderstanding motivation, and sometimes taking those misunderstandings much too personally.

Everyone is different; some people approach the world from a logical standpoint and some people focus on values and harmony first. Some people think and then speak. Some people speak and then think. Some need closure and make quick decisions. Others want to keep their possibilities open.

Given that there are several personality type inventories and indicators available to the general public, and given that you may have experience with any one of them or none of them, I expanded on the old adage, "Is your glass half empty or half full?" as a way to explain some of the personalities you might work with. The image of a half-empty glass or a half-full glass represents personality types in terms of their attitude toward a task or concept. My goal here is to plant seeds that may grow into a better understanding of how personalities impact our communication and blossom into a desire to learn more.

Personality types go beyond optimistic and pessimistic. There are so many nuances to the human personality that we could spend our lives learning about them. However, we work with a variety of personalities all day, every day, so we can only benefit when we understand personality types and how to address them.

Full Glass, Empty Glass Personality Types

Glass #1: "You call that a glass of water? Well, back where I come from…"

Are you working with someone who might say that?

Or, "It's half-empty now, and it wouldn't surprise me if it dried up completely."

Or, "Hey! Whose job was it to fill up this glass?"

If your co-teacher is this personality type, how might you present material so that she's comfortable with your approach? One approach she may be comfortable with is outlining. Presenting information through outlines is a traditional method of presenting information. It's a very effective teaching strategy for verbal linguistic and linear thinkers. However, it is not the best approach for visual learners who need to see information connected in terms of the whole in order to understand.

What approach might you use when working with a co-teacher who not only values tradition, but also thinks in concrete, linear terms?

I'm a learning strategy specialist, so I might add a graphic organizer to an outline and call it an addendum. I wouldn't expect my co-teacher to throw out the outline and adopt my way of teaching. Rather, I understand the value of providing both tools in the classroom so we will reach more student learning styles.

So our choices are an outline, or an outline plus a graphic organizer. What does this have to do with personality types? If someone has always done a task one way and you offer an alternative, you are going to have to do some convincing. Different personality types will respond in different ways to your efforts.

When she says "Back where I come from..." what she really means is, "Where's the data? It always worked this way; why change it now?" When working with this personality type, present a strategy you know will work when you present it. Show your partner the data that validates the use of strategies such as graphic organizers and nonlinguistic representation and shows that they increase achievement. When she says, "Back in my day..." give her what she needs; show her that your ideas work and indicate how they can save time.

If your partner says, "It's half-empty now and it wouldn't surprise me if it dried up completely," she needs you to demonstrate how your ideas benefit the students. She might ask, "Where's the benefit in doing this? Where's the benefit in the graphic organizer? Why should I change what I'm doing to use that?" Tell her why. Show her the statistics to back up your suggestions and how results can be measured.

If you believe your co-teacher might respond to the question "Is your glass half-empty or half-full?" with the response, "Whose job is it to fill up this glass?" then answer his questions. If he has a lot of questions, don't take offense and think it's because he's grilling you or doesn't trust you. It's because his learning style makes it necessary for him to understand why he's doing whatever he's doing. Once he understands, you can usually get him on board.

Glass #2: "I can't believe someone would leave that dirty glass out here! Clean this mess up right now!"

Do you work with this person? "Who left the mess in the classroom? Why do you keep your desk such a mess?" This person needs to have his ducks all in a row. Your mission with this co-teacher is to provide tools and forms that support the structure necessary for students to be successful in the classroom.

This personality type insists on practical, usable results. "Show me how it will clearly benefit me and my students." Share approaches and techniques that provide immediate results.

Glass # 3 "Hmm...It's (ingeniously constructs a hacksaw from two straws and a shoelace and cuts the glass in half)... Ah...Now it's completely full!"

You may work with a teacher who can go hog-wild with solutions, mnemonics, crazy different strategies, and different ways of doing things.

This is the personality type who can do things no one else can. When presenting options, accommodations, or adaptations to this co-teacher, express how the teaching method you want to implement will increase the competency of the students in the classroom. This personality type is a problem-solver, a troubleshooter who values competence above all else. Make sure this co-teacher understands that your intent is not simply to make students feel good; rather, it's to help them grow and succeed on their tests. Make proficiency the criteria and if it works, go for it.

Glass #4: "Hey!!! I bet if we got a bunch of these glasses, we could make a waterslide! Or maybe a pool! Oh wait, we could freeze this water and make an ice sculpture! Or we could..."

Do you work with this person? She's always coming up with a new random idea and never knows what's going to be in the lesson plan that day. "Because, you know, if something more exciting comes along, that's what we're going to be doing. To heck with the lesson plan."

Bruce was that kind of personality and the students loved him. Science with Bruce was fun. I, on the other hand, was totally frustrated with the lack of discipline in the classroom. Students were all over the place, talking and not paying attention. I struggled because I felt the students did not show appropriate respect for Bruce or their learning.

Bruce and I discussed student behavior during one of our planning meetings, which gave me the opportunity to suggest that I might assist with discipline. He was perfectly fine with me being the disciplinarian while he remained the storyteller. We worked well together that way. As long as he backed me up, I was the one who maintained control in the classroom and Bruce was the one who came up with all the great, spontaneous ideas.

I put the structure around Bruce's lecture on the white board and the chalkboard. I did the outlines and the graphic organizers and he told his stories. Again, the students loved him.

This personality type develops relationships and fosters student growth. Bruce cared about the rapport with his students more than anything else. Yes, he wanted them to learn, but he believed that they would learn if they had a positive relationship with him. When working with a co-teacher who approaches teaching like Bruce, indicate how your teaching suggestions will promote student accomplishment. Bruce's priority is caring about his students and maintaining harmony in the classroom. Focus on his and others' giftedness. He loved it when students came up with creative, out-of-the-box things. Make learning fun.

When we're working with different personality types, we have to be flexible. Think about your strengths and how they can complement your co-teacher's strengths. Adopt the philosophy, "They are all our students." I would also recommend that you research personality styles. My efforts to understand personality types have made a huge difference for me and for my teaching relationships.

When in Conflict

There are times in the classroom when there will be conflicts. How does a person handle conflict in a constructive way? How does a person manage the relationship so that both can work together without offending or hurting each other? When situations get tough, one of the first things to do is remember that, when in conflict, it is most often about personality. The other person is usually not trying to "get you."

What are we thinking when something happens in the classroom that triggers our frustration or our anger? Often we are thinking such things as, "That person should know better." "I told her she should do such-and-such and she didn't listen to me!" "Every time this happens in the classroom, he does that simply to annoy me." "She's an idiot." "He thinks he knows everything!" Or, "She is a control freak. I can't stand her." These types of statements are examples of negative self-talk. Negative self-talk fosters more negativity, anger, frustration, and dissatisfaction.

What if we change our self-talk? What if, instead of saying, "This person is doing this to annoy me," we replace that thought with, "She's trying her best. This is just her personality. How might I approach this person who is so different from me in her approach to the world?" What if we simply say, "I can handle this!" Or, "This isn't about me. This is about him, and I need to know how to approach him."

When we can take a step back and look at situations in terms of personality, it is much easier to handle conflicts in the classroom. Instead of taking things personally, we understand that it is simply about personality and a person's comfort level.

Once you have your positive self-talk – for example, you have told yourself, "I can handle this!" – start considering solutions to the problem. Seek the counsel of a respected colleague or someone you know who really understands how to approach different personalities. You will find that person by looking for someone who seems to be able to work with just about anyone and who has an amazing understanding of people. Seek that person out and ask him or her how you might approach the problem. Ideally, you would do this without naming the individual with whom you are having a problem.

There are many resources available to help people figure out what to say. In a difficult situation, use these resources. Albert Ellis has several books on the market that share strategies for how to handle difficult situations and feelings, and suggest ways to keep our minds in a rational and positive place. For example, just the title of his book, "*How to Stubbornly Refuse to Make Yourself Miserable About Anything – Yes, Anything*" (Paperback - July 1988) encourages a smile.

Consider using "I" statements to share how you feel about a situation. Avoid using the word "you" when communicating how you feel. Be careful to avoid blaming language. Even if you believe the other person is wrong,

Reflection Notes

find a way to approach the conversation from a positive perspective. Once you figure out how you want to handle the problem, role-play a conversation with another trusted colleague or friend. Visualize the interaction in your mind. Practice what you will say until you feel confident. Visualize that you are successful in this interaction.

There are times when it is best to say nothing. That choice is more difficult for some personalities than others. There are times when it is important to speak up about our concerns, and that, too, is easier for some personalities and more difficult for others. The most critical factor is that whatever we choose to do, we try to frame our actions, our words, and our thoughts in positive ways.

When in Conflict

1. Change negative self-talk to positive.

2. Consider "Next time X happens, I'll do Y or Z."

3. Plan viable solutions.

4. Consider personality type.

5. Seek suggestions from a supportive colleague or read Albert Ellis for suggestions to reframe.

6. Visualize yourself in the interaction ***Being Successful!***

7. Affirm: "I CAN handle this situation!"

What Can We Say? Scripts that Work

- What can I do to support you?
- How can I help make this challenge easier for you?
- Can we talk about something I think might help us work together better?
- I'd like to talk about...with you, but first I'd like to get your point of view.
- I think we may have different ideas about... I'd really like to hear your thinking on this and share my perspective as well.

Tone of voice...
Oh!
Oh?
Ohhhhh

When practicing and using these scripts, pay attention to your tone of voice. Be certain there is no hint of sarcasm in your tone. Be calm, cool and collected and be careful not to move into the other person's personal space.

The one- or two-syllable response	
Statement:	Sample Responses
I can't possibly see how co-teaching will work.	• Really? • I see • Oh...

Ask a question	
Statement:	Sample Responses
This activity is inappropriate for...	What do you mean by "inappropriate"? (Have research available)

Agree in part and ask a question	
Statement:	Sample Responses
This won't work without time to plan.	You are right. We have no common planning time. What can we do to make the best of our situation?

Agree and insist (Don't say, "but...")	
Statement:	Sample Responses
I have my way of doing things. I can't see how we can work together – we are so different!	I would say the same thing if I were you. And we still have the problem of being assigned to this...

Stopping Conflict in Its Tracks

Have you ever had people in your life who seem to enjoy baiting you? Have you wondered if all of their amusement in life comes from trying to get a rise out of you? Have you ever found yourself in a conversation with a colleague and, when the conversation finished, you shook your head and asked yourself what that was all about? Have you ever thought, "I should have said this!" and "I should have said that"? Often we leave the conversations feeling defeated and strangely so, because we are not always sure what happened.

Do you have someone you interact with who seems to have an answer for everything? What about someone who happens to be overly critical? How do we handle these types of conversations and these characters in our lives who challenge us with their words? Consider learning and using words and phrases that stop conflict in its tracks.

I remember a colleague of mine who was in the business world for his entire career. He loved to jibe me about being a teacher. Every time we got together, he would disparage the teaching profession. He knew I was a teacher and he loved to see my reaction. Of course, much to his pleasure, I reacted in passionate defense. Year after year, however, this became a tiresome tradition when we visited. Finally, one day, my colleague started in with his tirade about teaching and teachers in the profession and I simply looked at him with a smile on my face and said, "You have an interesting perspective. I'll have to give that more thought." Then I changed the subject. Much to my amazement, his jaw dropped and he seemed to search for what to say next. It took the wind out of his sails, and it was done so nicely.

Knowing phrases that stop conflict in its tracks is just one piece of the conflict-avoidance puzzle. The words we speak are actually less than 10% of our total communication. Body language and tone of voice are critical factors in how we communicate with other people. Body language communicates more than 80% of what we are trying to express. Tone of voice communicates more than 10% of what we are trying to convey. So if we have a comeback that should diffuse a conflict situation, such as "You have an interesting perspective. I'll have to give that some thought," the body language we use when we say those words and the tone of voice with which we speak them could render them either fighting words or words that diffuse a conflict situation. A calm and neutral tone of voice and relaxed body language will be the key factors as to whether the words actually stop conflict in its tracks.

When you find yourself caught in a verbal exchange that does not 'feel' right, then you may be dealing with bullying – intimidation, bulldozing, sarcasm, pushiness, exploitation, manipulation, etc.

You may also simply be dealing with someone who is upset over a misunderstanding and unable to communicate clearly in the moment.

1. <u>Recognize & pay attention</u> to your body signals; don't ignore the discomfort, adrenaline rush, etc.

2. <u>Stop, breathe & think</u>: "I CAN handle this!" (Positive self-talk)

3. <u>Consciously act</u>! (As opposed to re-act.)

Be conscious of your body language and the words you choose: Keep Your Power!

Comebacks that don't escalate the conflict

<ul><li>I see.</li><li>Thank you for letting me know how you feel.</li><li>Perhaps you are right.</li><li>I hear you.</li><li>Ouch! (Cues the other person that they are being hurtful. Sometimes they don't realize.)</li><li>I can see this upsets you.</li><li>I'm sorry you were hurt. That was not my intent.</li><li>I shouldn't have to defend myself, and I won't.</li><li>Excuse me, I'm not finished. (Say softly.)</li><li>Agree with some of the statement but not all. (e.g. "You have a chip on your shoulder because you are short." Agree. Say, "Yes, I am short.")</li><li>You have an interesting perspective.</li><li>I'll have to give that some thought.</li><li>I will talk to you when you are calm. (Call "Time" & leave)</li><li>I will talk to you when I am calm. (Call "Time" & leave)</li></ul>	Ask a question- S/he who asks the questions has the power. <ul><li>Why does that bother you?</li><li>How so?</li><li>Why do you ask?</li><li>What makes you say that?</li><li>I know you wouldn't have said that unless you had a good reason. Could you tell me what it was?</li></ul>

Tips for Success

Be careful about tone of voice and/or lower your voice. Avoid "should," "ought," and "you" statements. Watch your body language. Respect personal space.

Reflection Notes

Tips for Successful Collaboration

- Be flexible.
- Look for success not only in academic areas.
- Make time to plan – even if just 10 minutes.
- Discuss problems only with each other.
- Avoid using red ink to write notes to your colleague.
- Make sure your co-teacher understands that that you respect and value his opinions and his teaching strategies.

Pick-Me-Ups, Pick-U-Ups

- Compliment your colleague where all can see.
- Send a letter of appreciation and cc the principal.
- Remember special days with cards.

Something to think about

In my professional experience, the most effective way to meet the needs of students on an IEP in the general classroom is to seek out ways the general classroom teacher can implement adaptations quickly and easily. An adaptation that works for all students in the classroom and does not reduce content will more likely be embraced. Consequently, <u>all</u> students benefit. Simply embracing this belief will be the foundation of co-teaching success.

Communication: What's Working Card

Reflection Notes

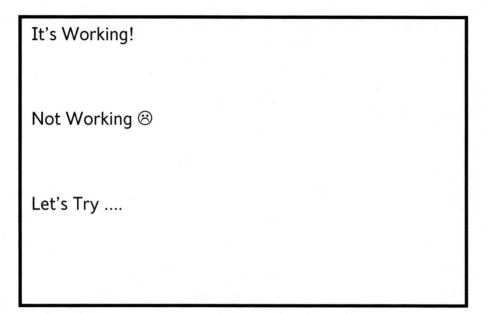

It's Working!

Not Working ☹

Let's Try ....

Good communication with coworkers and students is critical to successful inclusion. Often, our fears, agendas, and even enthusiasm get in the way of doing the kind of listening we need to do to foster good communication. Without effective communication, we make many assumptions about the people with whom we interact. Those assumptions might be very inaccurate and create tremendous conflict. Try to keep an open mind. Express how you feel and listen to hear other points of view. Good communication is necessary for the success of an inclusive classroom.

This card is a simple way to give feedback to your co-workers or individual members of the teaching team. I found it to be useful for reinforcing the positives. It can be delivered in person, or placed in a teacher mailbox. Simple 3 x 5 index cards work well.

Appendix: Tools and Supports

Readability Formulas

SMOG Readability Formula

The SMOG formula is a recommended and tested method for grading the readability of written materials. The method is quick, simple to use and particularly useful for shorter materials, e.g., a study's information pamphlet or consent form. To calculate the SMOG reading level, begin with the entire written work being assessed and follow these steps:

1. Count off 10 consecutive sentences near the beginning, in the middle, and near the end of the text. If the text has fewer than 30 sentences, use as many as are provided.
2. Count the number of words containing 3 or more syllables (polysyllabic), including repetitions of the same word.
3. Look up the approximate grade level on the SMOG conversion table below:

Total Polysyllabic Word Count	Approximate Grade Level (+1.5 Grades)
1-6	5
7-12	6
13-20	7
21-30	8
31-42	9
43-56	10
57-72	11
73-90	12
91-110	13
111-132	14
133-156	15
157-182	16
183-210	17
211-240	18

For more info including Spanish formulas:
http://www.cdc.gov/OD/ads/smog.htm

When using the SMOG formula:

- A sentence is defined as a string of words punctuated with a period, an exclamation mark, or a question mark. Consider long sentences with a semi-colon as two sentences.
- Hyphenated words are considered as one word.
- Numbers, which are written, should be counted. If written in numeric form, they should be pronounced to determine if they are polysyllabic.
- Proper nouns, if polysyllabic, should be counted.
- Abbreviations should be read as though unabbreviated to determine if they are polysyllabic. However, abbreviations should be avoided unless commonly known.

If the written piece being graded is shorter than 30 sentences, approach it as follows:

- Count all of the polysyllabic words in the test.
- Count the number of sentences.
- Find the average number of polysyllabic words per sentence, i.e.:

Total # of polysyllabic words
Average = Total # of sentences

- Multiply that average by the average number of sentences *short* of 30.
- Add that figure on to the total number of polysyllabic words.
- Compare the number of polysyllabic words in the SMOG conversion table.

For the Fry Readability Formula see:
http://school.discovery.com/schrockguide/fry/fry.html

To display readability statistics in MSWord (These instructions are for MSWord 2000):

On the Tools menu, click 'Options', and then click the 'Spelling & Grammar' tab.
Select the 'Check grammar with spelling' checkbox.
Select the 'Show readability statistics' checkbox, then click 'OK'.
Click 'Spelling and Grammar' on the Standard toolbar.
When Word finishes checking spelling and grammar, it displays information about the reading level of the document.

Acknowledgment Dr. Mary S. Neumann, DHAP, NCHSTP, "Developing Effective Educational Print Materials"

NOTE: In MSWord 2007 Spelling and Grammar tools are customized under the Word Options tool in the main drop down menu.

1. Click on the MS ball in the upper left corner.
2. Click on 'Word Options' at the bottom of the dropdown box.
3. Click on 'Proofing'.
4. At the bottom of the menu box, click on 'Show readability statistics'.

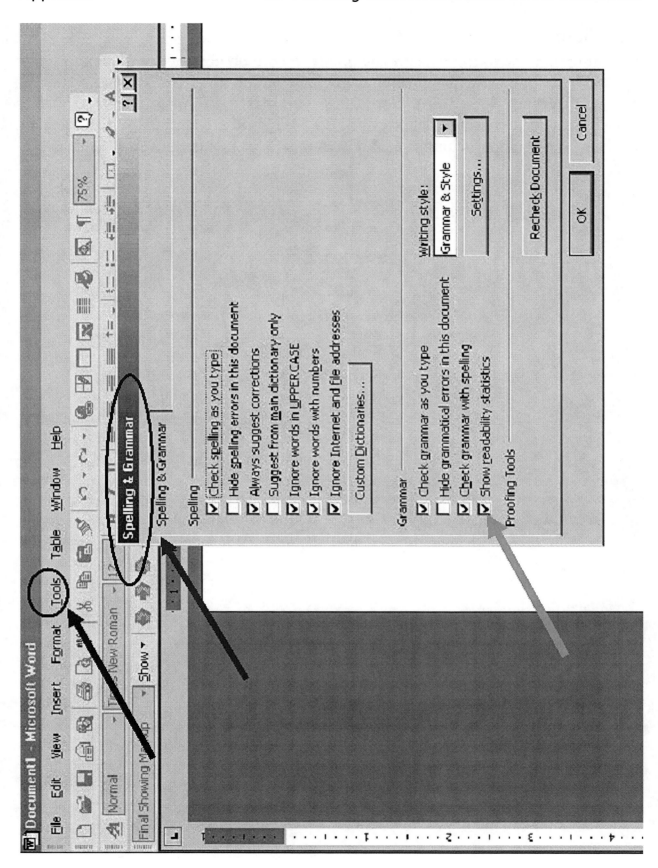

AutoSummarize in MSWord

Use AutoSummarize to highlight key points, create an abstract or a summary of a student's writing. Use it to summarize information that is too long for some students to read. **Note: In MSWord 2007**, you must add 'Autosummary Tools' to your customized shortcut ribbon. Click on 'Help' and search for "Autosummary". Choose "Automatically Summarizes a Document" for instructions.

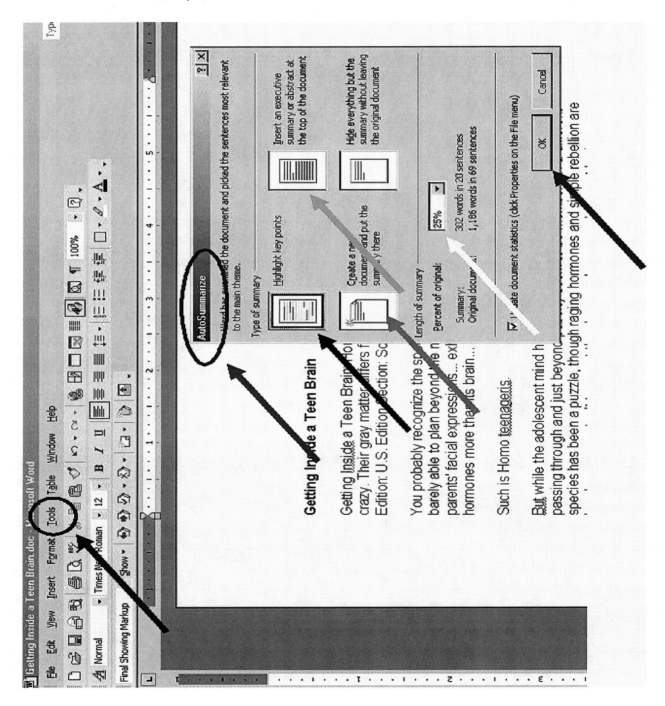

Homework

Homework is a constant challenge for teachers, students, and parents. Consider that homework requires support at home that many students do not have. Some students are going home to work after school to support themselves or their families. Many youth are on their own for homework. Given that reality, homework should be do-able. The following suggestions can make homework more manageable.

- Give students a choice of two assignments and allow them to pick which one they believe will help them the most.
- Give homework that goes "backwards" to make up skills students missed and homework that "challenges" for students who have the current lesson down.
- Set up a "homework checkers" system. If there are two or three different homework assignments, have kids get into groups of like assignments and check their answers. Beside each answer they check, they write, "We think this answer is right because..."
- Check to see who has their homework done. Those who don't have their homework done go a separate place in the room do their homework while the other students check each other's homework.
- Use homework rubrics. See examples on the next page.
- Rather than assigning worksheets or summary questions for homework, have students create:
  - Mnemonics.
  - Content written into a song (think grammar rock).
  - Rhymes for remembering facts and concepts taught in the lesson.
  - Cartoons, comic strips, or snapshot devices that illustrate content. Share these with the rest of the class so that all can remember content.
  - Vocabulary cartoons.
  - Mind maps and graphic organizers from text content.
  - Illustrated flash cards.

Homework Rubrics

OPTION ONE

Performance Descriptor	1	2	Points Earned
Heading			
Timeliness (On time)			
Effort			
Accuracy			
Neatness			
			Total:

OPTION TWO

Name, Date, Period on Upper right	1	
Neat	1	
Title at Top	1	
Completion/Effort	3	
Accuracy	3	
Parent/Support Person Signature	1	
Total Possible Points	10 points	Points Earned:

OPTION THREE

Heading (Name, date, period, assignment)	1	
Neat	1	
On time	1	
Completeness & effort		
All-most-some-none	4	
Correctness		
All-most-some-none	4	
Work shown (support answers)		
All-most-some-none	4	
Total Possible Points	15 points	Points Earned:

OPTION FOUR

Assignment	0-No HW	1- Attempted incomplete	2- Skills applied complete/late	3- Complete on time

Bibliography

Bacharach, N and Heck,T and Dahlberg, K (2005). "Improving Student Academic Achievement using a Co-Teaching Model of Student Teaching" 1-37. Web.29 Aug 2009. <http://www.teachercenter.mnscu.edu/staff/featured/JTEpiece.pdf>.

Dean, Stacy Pellechia (2007). Lesson Plan Book for the Diverse Classroom. Port Chester, NY: Dude Publishing.

Dieker, L (2002). The Co-Teaching Lesson Plan Book. Whitefish Bay, WI: Knowledge by Design, Inc.

Fitzell, S (2007). Special Needs in the General Classroom: Strategies that Make it Work! Manchester, NH: Cogent Catalyst Publications.

Friend, M (1999). Successful Co-Teaching Strategies. Seattle, WA: Bureau of Education & Research.

Marzano, R (2001). Classroom Instruction that Works. Alexandria, VA: ASCD.

Villa, R (2004). A Guide to Co-Teaching. Thousand Oaks, CA: Corwin Press.

MidValley Consortium for Teacher Education, (2000). Partners for Student Achievement; A Co-Teaching Resource Handbook. VA: Virginia DOE.

Order Susan's Books!

Cogent Catalyst Publications

an AIMHI Educational Programs partner company

Customer information

Name: _____

Street: _____

City, State & Zip: _____

Phone 1: _____

Phone 2: _____

Email Address: _____

Order Date:

Mail orders to PO Box 6182, Manchester, NH 03018 or Fax to (603) 218-6291 * Contact us at info@cogentcatalyst.com * 603-625-6087

Shipping & Handling

Order Total	Shipping Price
Up to $55.00 (except P	Free Shipping
Large posters (< 10)	$7.95
$55.01 - $70.00	$9.95
$70.01 - $100.00	$11.95
$100.01 - 149.00	$13.95
More than $149.01	10% of Subtotal

All orders are shipped via USPS and can be expected within 14 days of the time we receive your order. Items ordered at one time are shipped together whenever possible.

Qty.	Description	Unit Price	Discounted/Bulk Price	Line Total
	Co-Teaching and Collaboration in the General Classroom 2nd Ed.	$24.97		
	Set of 10: Co-Teaching and Collaboration		$199.97	
	Free the Children: Conflict Education for Strong, Peaceful Minds	$15.95		
	Set of 10: Free the Children		$124.97	
	Paraprofessionals and Teachers Working Together 2nd Edition	$24.97		
	Set of 10: Paraprofessionals and Teachers		$199.97	
	Please Help Me With My Homework: English 2nd Edition	$10.97		
	Set of 10: Please Help Me		$87.97	
	Please Help Me With My Homework: Spanish	$10.97		
	Set of 10: Please Help Me		$87.97	
	Special Needs in the General Classroom 2nd Edition	$24.97		
	Set of 10: Special Needs		$199.97	
	Transforming Anger to Personal Power	$23.95		
	Set of 10: Transforming Anger		$199.97	
	Umm Studying? What's That?	$15.00		
	Set of 10: Umm Studying?		$119.97	
	Memorization & Test Taking Strategies DVD Training Program	$895.00		
	Flash Cards: Special Needs in the General Classroom	$7.95		
	Flash Cards: Umm Studying... What's That?	$7.95		
	Poster- MOODZ: Laminated 8 1/2" x 11"	$4.95		
	Poster-MOODZ: Gloss Coverstock 18" x 24"	$9.95		
	Poster-Feed The Future One Drop at a Time 15" X 11" (standard size)	$9.95		
	Poster Set-Response to Intervention	$29.95		
	Resource CD: Ready-Made Forms & Tools 2010	$9.95		
	Sticky Notes "Best Ideas"	$2.50		
	Write-In:			
	Write-In:			
	Write-In:			
			Subtotal:	
			Shipping & Handling:	
			Total:	

****Large posters require shipping because of tube mailers**

The portion below must be filled out or your order will not be processed

☐Cash　　　　☐Check　　　　☐Visa/MC

Visa/MC#_____　　　　Exp.Date: _____

Make checks payable to Susan Fitzell

Bright Ideas

_____

_____

_____

_____

_____

_____

_____

_____

_____

_____

_____

_____